THINK LIKE A CHAMPION

THINK LIKE A CHAMPION

MIKE SHANAHAN
with ADAM SCHEFTER

HarperBusiness
A Division of HarperCollins*Publishers*

HarperCollins books may be purchased for educational, business, or sales promotional use. For information please write: Special Markets Department, HarperCollins Publishers, Inc., 10 East 53rd Street, New York, NY 10022.

FIRST EDITION

Designed by William Ruoto

Library of Congress Cataloging-in-Publication Data

Shanahan, Mike.
Think like a champion : building success one victory at a time / Mike Shanahan and Adam Schefter. —1st ed.
p. cm.
ISBN 0-06-662039-2
1. Shanahan, Mike. 2. Football coaches—United States—Biography. 3. Sports—Psychological aspects. I. Schefter, Adam. II. Title.
GV939.S419A3 1999
796.332'092—dc21

99-32823

99 00 01 02 03 ❖/RRD 10 9 8 7 6 5 4 3 2 1

To Peggy—for the commitment, dedication, and sacrifice to make all this possible.

—Mike Shanahan

To Nanny Blanche and Poppy Dave—for saving a spot on your bookshelf long before this project was an idea.

—Adam Schefter

CONTENTS

TESTIMONIALS

PREGAME TALK

Let's get one thing straight right now, before we go any further: If I can achieve the level of success I have, you can, too.

Look at me. I'm just another midwestern guy from another blue-collar family in Franklin Park, Illinois—making me the considerably lesser-known Mike from Chicago—in a position I could not have envisioned or imagined as a kid. I didn't go to some academic institution like Harvard or some football factory like Michigan. It was little-known Eastern Illinois, out on the plains of Charleston, Illinois, about 200 miles south of Chicago.

Eastern Illinois was an easy choice. It was the only school that offered me a full football scholarship. If I hadn't had a full scholarship offer, I wouldn't have had the money to go to college. But off I went, and I almost didn't live to tell about it.

During my junior year there in 1974, during the annual spring game in which I was playing quarterback, I ran an option play that didn't have too many options. In fact, there was only one: running right at a linebacker. As I pitched the football, raising my right arm and leaving my side exposed, he speared me where I was suddenly vulnerable.

From that point on, every breath was a struggle, yet I somehow managed to finish the game. But when our team headed out to celebrate the end of spring practice, as it did each year, I returned to my apartment instead. I felt awful.

When I went to the bathroom, I urinated bright red. Then I began vomiting profusely, my gut twisting and clenching. I filled up the sink three times before one of my roommates called the school's trainer, who called an ambulance. Moments later, I was being rushed to the emergency room at Charleston Hospital.

The emergency room doctors gave me all kinds of x-rays. They couldn't find anything wrong, but if the pain was any indication, I knew something was very wrong. I pleaded with the doctors to keep searching. If there was any skepticism on their part, it disappeared when I passed out, my vital signs went, and my heart actually stopped beating for thirty seconds.

After the doctors managed to resuscitate me, I immediately underwent emergency surgery, during which it was discovered that one of my kidneys had been split open. The reason it failed to show up on the x-rays was because after it was jarred loose, it was hidden behind my vertebrae. Once the doctors were able to find the ruptured kidney, they removed it.

Still, the situation was dire. A priest was summoned to administer the last rites. And when my father arrived at the hospital that night at about nine o'clock, after his three-hour drive from Franklin Park, the priest met him in the parking lot with news no parent wants to hear. It didn't look like I would make it.

But after five days in critical condition, to everyone's surprise, my condition was upgraded. As I became more aware, the tubes gradually were removed, my color progressively returned, and I slowly began to feel like myself again. One doctor later told my father it was the closest he had ever come to losing a patient who actually survived. But the ramifications were severe—life-changing.

After it became clear I would live, Eastern Illinois's football coach, Jack Dean, walked into my hospital room and told me my football-playing days were over. That was it. Done. Neither the doctors nor the school could allow me to play again. I was crushed. I should have been thankful I was alive, but all I could think about was never playing football again.

I tried to petition the school to allow me back onto the playing field, only to have my request denied. What would I do now? How could I get past this life-altering obstacle and go from surviving to thriving? My mother, a housewife, would have liked for me to become a fireman. My father, an electrician, would have liked for me to join him in his field. But football, with all due respect to my parents, had become my life. Now that I couldn't play, I needed to find some other way to stay involved in the game. As a kid, I always aspired to be a coach. I just didn't realize that my career in that field would be getting started so soon.

Coaching—that shows you how smart I was back then. As a coach, you've got to be an assistant for about fifteen years, get paid next to nothing for working around the clock, move your family all over the country, have almost no life, sacrifice it all for the chance to one day get ulcers, and maybe even be fired. But it was something I wanted very badly. And in my mind, the only way to do it was to go armed with a plan.

If I was going to be a coach, I wanted to be the best, and that clearly meant seeking out the top coaches and programs and learning from them. With that plan, avoiding mistakes becomes more likely. Then success becomes that much more achievable.

I always relate it to buying your first car. You go in there, you want to strike a deal on your own, you bargain as best as you can with the salesman. He's telling you he'll give you $1,000 off the sticker price, and he's got an insurance agent already lined up for you, and the car is ready to be driven out of the showroom.

"What a deal!" you think. You take it.

Then you look back fifteen years later, after you've already bought three cars, and you laugh at yourself and how stupid you were. You realize that even though the salesman said he had to go into the back room, he had to talk to his boss, he had to do all this so he could haggle to get a better price for you, he really didn't do any such thing at all. But he made you feel like he was doing you some kind of big favor.

Yeah, right. He took you for a ride before you owned the car.

But that's sales. And that's experience. Of course, if you had talked to someone who already had gone through the process or consulted someone who actually works in car dealerships—like, say, John Elway—the outcome would have been different.

In whatever endeavor you are in, it takes an intelligent person to thoroughly investigate the pitfalls, seek the keys to advancement, and realize what it is that separates the ordinary people from the extraordinary people. Is it preparation? Sacrifice? Luck? What? When I was younger, I didn't know. Shortly after receiving my B.A. in the spring of 1975, I set out to find out.

My journey as a coach started in Norman, Oklahoma, home of the University of Oklahoma Sooners, which was at that time one of the country's finest football programs. My friends and family told me I was half-crazy for moving out there without knowing anyone and without having any job other than being the resident assistant of a dormitory.

I didn't care. I had a plan. Each day, without invitation, I would leave the dorm and visit the Oklahoma football office, the locker room, the film room. I would ask the assistant coaches if they needed any odd jobs done, and inevitably they'd have something for me to do. Some days I would shuttle recruits or coaches back and forth from the airport. Other days I would help break down game film or even chart plays. Before too long, they realized I was a worker.

As I alleviated them from their tedious tasks, the assistant coaches gradually grew accustomed to seeing me around the complex. They even allowed me to sit in on some coaching staff meetings. And when the team posed for its annual team picture in August and I stood off to the side watching everyone assemble for the cameraman, running backs coach Donnie Duncan called out to the Sooners head coach, Barry Switzer, "Hey, Barry, let's get Mike in this picture."

Barry looked over, recognized me from all the time I spent around the team, and yelled as he motioned me over, "Hey, Coach Mike, come here." Barry had no idea what my last name was, but that didn't matter to me. What mattered was that I was some microscopic part of Oklahoma's 1975 national championship team, a lowest-on-the-totem-pole assistant coach in one of the sport's best instructional laboratories.

After going to Oklahoma for a part-time resident assistant's job, I left two years later in 1977 at the age of twenty-four for a full-time backfield coaching job at Northern Arizona—a great chance for more learning. Just as people told me I shouldn't go to Oklahoma, they also told me I shouldn't leave Northern Arizona after the 1977 season to take the offensive coordinator job at my alma mater, Eastern Illinois.

There was some talk that the school was going to drop its football program, particularly since it hadn't had a winning season in seventeen years. Twenty-one of its twenty-two players from the team that finished 1–10 the previous season were returning for the next season. They were the laughingstock of the state.

But why let the past determine the future? With an expanded coaching role for me and with new leadership in place—Eastern Illinois had hired former University of Arizona and Florida State head coach Darrell Mudra, who, for good reason, was nicknamed "Dr. Victory"—it was time to believe anything was possible.

At our first team meeting after I accepted the job at Eastern, Darrell walked into the room with a simple, yet hard-to-believe message.

"Men," he told our players and coaching staff, "you are going to be winners. I've looked at a lot of film and know the talent we have and I know we will get to the [Division II] playoffs with the right plan and right attitude. There is no reason why we cannot win a national championship."

Everybody looked at him as if he was on drugs, including me. I thought we definitely could win, but he was talking about a national championship when we hadn't had a winning record in nearly twenty years. But at the end of the season, he was right. We had a 12–2 record. We set twenty-five school records. Our offense averaged 424.6 yards and 35 points per game.

And we won the national championship.

In a town of maybe 7,000 people, 12,000 greeted us when we came back to town with the trophy. And now that I look back on it, I shouldn't have been surprised at all. Coach Mudra had a vision and he would not be denied.

There were concepts and ideas and philosophies I observed everywhere I went. And over time I discovered that winning wasn't just limited to the football field. When I spent three seasons with the San Francisco 49ers, I found out that their former coach and current general manager Bill Walsh used to go into the Silicon Valley to speak to the biggest computer companies out there. They would pepper Bill with football questions, and he would pepper them with business questions. They would use his ideas, and he would use theirs.

How did the 49ers win five Super Bowls in fifteen years? Well, some of it was due to the same principles that Bill Gates utilized to become one of our country's most successful and richest entrepreneurs. Set your goals. Believe you can achieve them. Maintain a positive attitude. Understand the team concept. Plan, sacrifice, compete, communicate, finish.

It is not easy. Achieving success never is. For me, it meant following a nomadic trail that took me from Eastern Illinois, to Oklahoma, to Northern Arizona, back to Eastern Illinois, to Minnesota, to Florida, to Denver, to Los Angeles, back to Denver, to San Francisco, and back to Denver again.

There were a lot of obstacles to overcome, a lot of mountains to climb. But after three Super Bowl wins in the past five seasons—one as the 49ers offensive coordinator in 1994 and two as the head coach of the Denver Broncos in 1997 and 1998—I found some indisputable answers that were not served up in any motivational pamphlets or inspirational books when I started out in my chosen profession at the age of twenty-two.

But now, after more than a quarter-century of coaching, after studying under some brilliant coaches, after coaching a number of successful players, I've been able to weave together these influential stories and unforgettable lessons. My hope is that the knowledge I've compiled will help you take some real steps toward success. My hope is that these words can help bring out the best in you.

There is no reason why they can't. Each professional field and each professional endeavor has its own jargon, but the language of winning is universal. You, too, can be a champion in your field, no matter how elusive that goal has been up to this point. Simply formulate a plan, apply it to your job, and be the best you can in your profession. Instead of just dreaming great dreams, you will wake up and figure out how to make them come true.

Some people might say, "Oh, sure, it's easy enough for you to prescribe these things. Your job is going well, you're financially secure, your world is super." In 1988, when I was thirty-five years old, it wasn't. I had just been selected as the head coach of the Los Angeles Raiders and I had to get an advance on my salary to put down on a house because we had no money. None. Zero. Any money we had saved had been used on moving from one job to the next. So I know as well as anyone. It takes years and years to make an overnight success.

You might as well get started now. It's never too late. That's what this book is here to help you do. My hope is that it will help you find your hidden powers. Sometimes you might not even realize they are there, but they are. You'll be surprised at how simple they can be to get at, and how much they can help you achieve greater results on your job, in your school, or in your sport. Hey, if somebody like me can do it, there's no reason you can't, too.

Of course, there is a little caveat. As Sean Connery said to Kevin Costner in *The Untouchables,* "What are you prepared to do?"

When I started out, I was prepared to drive the miles, to fight the enemies, to learn from role models. And when we tasted our first championship at Oklahoma in 1975, it wasn't enough; I wanted another. When we tasted my second national championship at Eastern Illinois as its offensive coordinator in 1978, it wasn't enough; I wanted another. And now that we've tasted two Super Bowl championships in two straight years in Denver and are aiming to becoming the first team in NFL history to win three straight Super Bowls, it's still not enough. It can't ever be.

There are always new challenges to face, personal and professional goals to achieve. Anyone who tastes success's sweetness would want more. And anyone with a second-to-none work ethic has a chance to achieve it. You might think, "Impossible, not me, someone else will get the sale or win the account." Why? Why not you?

I get so tired of listening to people say, "I wish." I call it "The Wish Syndrome," and we all hear it all the time. "I wish I played the piano. I wish I drove a nicer car. I wish I lived in a bigger house. I wish I had more money." That Wish Syndrome is a killer.

Don't wish for something. Go make it happen. You don't ever hear successful people wishing for something, do you? They make up their mind to go get it. There's no reason you can't do the same. It's not magic. It's about you.

In going about your job, there's a certain way to do it. I learned that early on. Growing up in Franklin Park, Illinois, my father made me clean out our garage every Saturday morning before I could go out and play with my friends. At first, I would just brush it out, make it look nice, do as little as it took to meet his satisfaction. When I was done, my dad would come into the garage, look around, shake his head, and tell me, "Not good enough."

So I'd clean another half-hour without working much harder. I'd call him in again, he'd look around, shake his head, and tell me, "Not good enough." After being rebuffed twice, I got mad and confrontational.

"What do you mean it's not good enough?" I would angrily ask him.

"Well," he would calmly tell me, "when you figure out how to do the job right, then you're free to go out and play."

From that moment on, each Saturday I would take everything out of the garage, hose it down, sweep it out, make sure there was not a speck of dirt in there. "He knows a job well done," I would think to myself, "so instead of going through the motions, I'm going to do this right so I don't have to do it again."

Those are the things you learn as a kid. Those are the things that still apply today. The only way to do a job is the right way. This is my plan for how to go about doing it.

So what are we waiting for? Let's get started.

EDWARD SHANAHAN

Mike Shanahan's Father

Fathers are supposed to be teaching their sons, not having their sons teach them. But sometimes when I talk to Mike, I feel like it's a learning experience for me.

He's got such insight into football and life. Sometimes I'll ask him how something is done, whether it's on the football field or off it, and he'll explain it in a way that makes perfect sense. It makes me feel like we have a walking, talking encyclopedia in the family.

When he was younger, he would be my summer helper, assisting me with my job as an electrician. In no time at all, I could see how perceptive he was. He picked up on everything, analyzing everything really well.

I often kid him now. I tell him if only he would have listened to me, he could have been an electrician. He could have made it in that field or really, now that I think about it, any field. If he had become an electrician like I wanted him to be, he wouldn't have won any Super Bowls, but he still would have made a pretty nice living.

But then, there was always something about the way this boy reacted to situations. When he started high school, I said, "Mike, it's quite obvious you're too small for football. You're just going to get yourself hurt." But he tried out anyway and he came home one day and said he made the freshman A team and I said, "Oh my God," because he weighed about 110 pounds at the time. I told myself, this kid is shocking me no matter what he does.

Much like a prizefighter, he just makes up his mind that he isn't going to lose, no matter what he competes in. He always has maintained that positive winning attitude, and it has carried him through in many cases. And it seemed like it has been that way throughout his whole life. Whenever I've thought, "Well, he's hit that plateau, he can't go much further," he'd bounce right back and do something to top that.

He has always felt that nothing could stop him. He always has put a lot of forethought into everything. Whatever he has done, he was totally prepared for, whether it was with playing football or anything else. Even when he was younger, he did a lot of thinking and reading, and I have to say that when I was his age, I never thought about preparation. It was just going out there to play and having a good time. But Mike always put that extra effort into it. That has always given him an edge.

His mother, Dorothy, is an awful lot like that, too. She is so thorough in her preparation, always planning ahead. I remember one time our daughter Joyce—who's now a lawyer—was writing an essay to try for a $1,000 scholarship. My wife had her make this outline, then modify it, and sure enough she won the scholarship. It was strictly through the aid of my wife breaking it down for her, showing her how to make it the best essay.

Mike carries that same quality. I think he picked up a lot from his mother. I had the competitive genes, she had the ones with preparation, and between the two of us, Mike got lucky. He got some of the best from both of us.

My wife and I often have said to each other that with what Mike has accomplished, it's a dream come true. But actually, to be honest, we never dreamt anything like this. I guess it just goes to show what one person can do.

1

PREPARING THE FOUNDATION

When we were in school, there were the things we enjoyed—making friends, being exposed to new ideas, learning from exceptional teachers. Then there were the things we hated—reading textbooks, writing term papers, pulling all-nighters. We figured, when we get out of school, that will be it. No more textbooks, no more term papers, no more final exams, no more homework.

But unfortunately, that is not it. That's not the way the world works. Even after school there is still more homework, albeit an altogether different kind.

Adult homework is preparation.

As far as I'm concerned, you can never do enough of it. Whatever endeavor you have entered, whatever field you have chosen, you should never walk into a business meeting without studying. Or a sales conference without researching. Or a theatrical play without rehearsing. Or a football game without practicing.

Otherwise, you're asking for a passport to failure.

Preparation is the foundation of this book, material that took forty-six years to research and three months to write. More important, it is the foundation of success.

The difference between someone who is successful and someone who isn't is not about talent. It's about preparation. So much of what successful people do—knowing the competition, making their luck, being equipped to take risks, overcoming adversity, dealing with success—is tied to the powerful principle of preparation. It enables people to move ahead, stay ahead, and live ahead. It is why, in this book, it bats leadoff, top of the order. Nothing you do is as important.

Through the years, what I've always learned, and always had reinforced, is that the way you go about your homework translates into the way you wind up performing. Being ready for any challenge in business or life provides the cross-hairs to take dead aim at the heart of success.

Compare it to selling a plot of land. If you haven't done all the possible research on it and the surrounding area, if you're not right on top of all the pertinent information, then you might struggle to close the deal. All of a sudden you're meeting with the buyer and he might say, "Hey, this lot that sold two miles down the road, what did it sell for?" If you don't know, you may have just lost the sale.

It's like I tell our team all the time: We have one chance to be successful on Sunday, and one chance only, and that is if we have the most thorough week of preparation possible. We start even with the competition on Sunday. But we get ahead of them Monday through Saturday.

When I was in San Francisco, some of those players had won three or four Super Bowls, yet they practiced at a premium level every day. Now we do the same in Denver. Other teams might feel like they can slack off from time to time, but with our team—with any winning team or organization—there is no other way. You have to practice at game speed. If you don't, then how do you expect to play perfectly on game day?

It is why our practices are demanding. We go through every conceivable situation and how we should respond. We work on visualization, going over every detail. We run each play 100 times in our minds. That way, whatever happens in the game, we've already seen before. If our team is facing a third down and 1 yard to go during the game and we have prepared for it during the week, we will be confident we are going to convert it.

We want our players to be so disciplined that their reaction is instinctive. No one can just wave a magic wand on Sunday, give a great pregame speech, and expect to go out there and win one for the Gipper. But if you approach things on a day-to-day basis, then you have a chance for greatness. And the only way to reach this level is to never let up. Always expecting the best forces you to operate at a higher level.

The other thing we do is run plays until we do it right. When I was in San Francisco, 49ers quarterback Steve Young used to call me "Mr. Let's Do It Again." But if we didn't run the play perfectly, the way it was supposed to be run during the game, sorry, but we were going to do it again.

We've adopted the same approach—but not nickname—in Denver. During our preparations for Super Bowl XXXIII against the Atlanta Falcons, the players felt like they had our game plan down just the way we wanted. It got to the point where the players were saying, "Get us away from these coaches! Let us just play already."

The Wednesday before the Super Bowl, we were crisp. Not once during practice did the ball touch the ground. We were in sync, we were in tune, every pass was right on the money. John Elway was conducting his orchestra like few things I have ever seen during my coaching career.

Watching John throw perfect pass after perfect pass, a memory hit me out of nowhere. I looked over to our offensive coordinator, Gary Kubiak, who was with me in San Francisco for the 1994 season, the year the 49ers won their fifth Super Bowl.

"Hey, Gary," I asked, sidling up next to him. "What does this remind you of?"

"Steve Young," Gary said. "That Thursday practice, boss."

That Thursday practice was when the 49ers were preparing for Super Bowl XXIX against the San Diego Chargers. We were crisp.

Not once during practice did the ball touch the ground. We were in sync, we were in tune, every pass was right on the money. Steve Young was conducting his orchestra like few things I had ever seen during my coaching career.

And Steve, just as we suspected he would, carried over his perfect preparation from Thursday to Sunday. He threw for an NFL-record six touchdown passes and was named MVP of Super Bowl XXIX, a 49–26 49ers win.

And John? He, too, carried over his perfect preparation from Wednesday to Sunday. In what turned out to be his final NFL game, he threw for 336 yards and was named MVP of Super Bowl XXXIII, a 34–19 Broncos win.

Funny how that works, but it always does. The way to bring out the best in you is not by chance, but rather through preparation.

Adult homework—as much as we all would rather not do it—does have its rewards.

Britain's former prime minister Winston Churchill often has been called the greatest orator of the twentieth century. People were amazed when he would give eloquent speeches without any notes. None. He would just go through his delivery as if he were improvising.

But later on, the truth was revealed. Churchill would spend all kinds of time, hours upon hours, rehearsing for his speeches in places no one could see. What appeared to be off-the-cuff brilliance was, in reality, nothing more than sheer preparation. Churchill did his homework.

It is no terrific secret. It is the same for greatness in any field. It's easy to say you're going to be prepared, but it's a harder thing to actually do. Getting the A in school, landing the big account, making the record sale, scoring the winning touchdown takes organization and determination—two essential components to preparation.

But if you're ready for your game, half the battle is already won.

Hey, we don't just go out on Sunday and play the game. Our coaching staff spends 100 hours per week in the office doing our own rigorous work, breaking down film, drawing up game plans, instructing our players. We script the first fifteen plays of each game, drawing them up for Sunday just like we plan to carry them out. It gives the players a chance to go through the first quarter the way it might unfold and understand what might happen. Anywhere from twenty-four to forty-eight hours before the game is played, players can start going through their mental routine, all the plays, defenses, and possible audibles and stunts they'll see.

Some people have asked me why I don't script a whole game. The reason? It's just not necessary. Fifteen plays gives me enough looks to let me know how the other team is defending us. Almost immediately, we get a good feel for what their defensive game plan is. Then, after the first fifteen plays, we revise our plan for the rest of the game. More often than not, it works. In the first quarter of the 1998 season, primarily using our fifteen scripted plays, we outscored our opponents 144–54.

Much of my individual preparation goes into a laminated play-calling sheet I carry with me on the sideline. What's on there is a good thirty hours of work per week—all the plays that I want to remind myself to use.

Back when I was coaching at Eastern Illinois and Minnesota and Florida, I would watch the film of our game on Monday morning and tell myself, "God, I should have done this or that." I would get different defenses and secondary coverages than I expected and did not have a written-out plan to refer to immediately. I told myself, from that point on, I had to have alternative plays readily available.

Once I got to the NFL, I began spending thirty hours per week writing down the plays, putting in writing what I needed to remember in certain game situations. What are we going to do on 4th-and-1 from the 33-yard line? What are we going to do on 1st-and–10 from midfield? What's the best play for any situation? I tried to cover every imaginable situation.

Each Sunday there are plays on my sheet we don't wind up using. But if we use only one idea from the sheet, and that one idea somehow helps us win, it's worth it.

Now, to design the sheet, which I do starting on Wednesday nights, I use all different-colored magic markers to code certain personnel groups. I will also write out the plays we might use in various situations: short yardage, red zone, third downs. On the sheet, it says "Must Calls" and "Mike's Reminders." Putting together the play-calling sheet each week is my homework. It's time-consuming, but it pays off.

Sometimes the plays I call will even come from play sheets I'd prepared early in the season. During Super Bowl XXXIII there was one play I used from the 8th week of our season. It was the "X Post," in which wide receiver Rod Smith is supposed to break outside and run a comeback route but instead breaks inside and runs a deep post route. On the sideline during the game, I huddled with Kubiak and Elway and told them, "They're dead. We've got a good play, especially if we're going against [Falcons cornerback Ronnie] Bradford."

Then, as I watched the Falcons line up in their defense—stacking the line of scrimmage in an attempt to slow down our running back Terrell Davis—I couldn't help myself from saying to anyone who would listen, "Oh, it's going to be wide open. It's going to be *wiiide* open."

And it was. The X Post proved to be the X factor. John rolled right, stopped, and threw deep down the middle of the field. Rod beat Falcons safety Eugene Robinson. The ball was right there, Rod pulled it in, and with 4:54 remaining in the first half, we had a touchdown and a commanding 17–6 lead.

Preparation paid profits.

It was the same thing in Super Bowl XXXII, the one we played a year earlier against the Green Bay Packers. As we were watching game film, we were like all the other teams that faced Green Bay. For the life of us, we could not figure out a way to stop, or even contain, the Packers outstanding Pro Bowl safety LeRoy Butler.

I'm telling you, we watched film for three straight days, around the clock, trying to devise some way to slow down this guy. We were consumed. No one could bother me during that time. I wouldn't even talk about Super Bowl ticket arrangements with my wife, Peggy, until I could come up with some way to bottle up Butler.

But on the third day we noticed something small. Every time a team lined up two wide receivers on the same side of the field and a Green Bay linebacker was covering the inside slot receiver, Butler would blitz. When a Green Bay cornerback was covering the inside slot receiver, Butler would cover the tight end man-to-man or drop into zone coverage, but we knew he wouldn't blitz. The formations would give away Butler's strategy.

Now, had we lined up in a balanced formation, with a wide receiver on each side of the field, we would have had no clue where Butler was coming from. He would have wreaked as much havoc as usual. But during the Super Bowl, we lined up Ed McCaffrey and Rod Smith on the same side of the field. And when John Elway stepped to the line of scrimmage and the Packers lined up defensively, he knew just what Green Bay and Butler were going to do on every play. John then was able to audible, getting us out of a bad play and into a good one.

Butler was completely neutralized in the game. We won 31–24. The reward for our long hours of preparation was our performance.

Out here in Colorado, or in any other area that has undergone any kind of dramatic population explosion, traffic and schools have become one big mess. Like the NFL's salary cap, it has gotten pretty tough to deal with.

Local authorities have approved growth far greater than the roads are designed to accommodate. It also is why too many children go to schools in temporary classrooms—otherwise known as aluminum trailers. City councils and county commissioners approved the growth, but they were unprepared for it. They didn't have a plan, not even a simple one.

Now they get failing grades for not doing their homework.

Here is your choice. You can have a plan or you can have the stress that comes along with not having one. Stress can destroy a lot of people. It can, in the long run, force you to retire or quit. But a well-thought-out plan will boost your confidence, your self-esteem, and your percentages for success. I don't care whether you're going against the Green Bay Packers or the largest computer manufacturer in the world, the only way to combat stress is to be prepared.

It's like taking a test in school. If you go into the test and you know the subject inside and out, you're going in there with a lot of confidence. If you go into that test and you don't know your subject inside and out, your stomach is in knots. There's no difference in football or life.

Now, don't go thinking I'm perfect. When we were playing the New York Giants last season with a chance to improve our record to 14–0 and move within two games of the only 16–0 regular-season finish in NFL history, I forgot to prepare our offense for one blitz the Giants ran occasionally. It was an oversight on my part, but it also was a source of stress the night before the game. I kept thinking about how I had failed to warn our offense and our fullback, Howard Griffith. I had this gnawing feeling that this one ounce of preparation we did not put our team through would cost us.

Sure enough, late in the fourth quarter, when we could have put away the game with one little first down, the Giants ran the one blitz I feared. Griffith was unable to pick it up. Terrell Davis was thrown for a loss, and after the Giants got back the ball and scored the game-winning touchdown, we had our first loss of the season.

That taught me a valuable lesson. From that point on, I vowed to myself that there would not be another play or sequence that our team would not be aware of as we kicked off our quest to repeat as Super Bowl champions. Some people might have thought we were not prepared the next week when we lost in Miami on a Monday night. In fact, it was just the opposite. We were preparing.

Having already locked up the AFC West title and home field advantage throughout the playoffs, we had nothing more to play for than pride. There was a decent chance we were going to play the Dolphins in an AFC divisional playoff game if they could beat us that Monday night.

So while they loaded up their playbook to get the win they desperately needed, we went with different looks out of our base offensive and defensive packages. The one set we did not use was one the New York Jets had a tremendous amount of success with versus Miami earlier in the season. We wanted to save that for a possible rematch three weeks later.

All I wanted to see was how the Dolphins aligned against various formations, how they matched up against our players and how they would defend us. I used the Monday night game as a preview, a coming attraction, a major form of preparing.

Now, would I tell our team that? No, of course I wouldn't. I wouldn't let them know that we didn't go in there with a full deck. That gives you an excuse if you lose, and people don't want to hear it. They want results. I told everybody from day one that we went in there with a full attack, and they got the job done and we didn't.

But I think our players sensed we held back when we handed out our game plan for our AFC divisional playoff against the Dolphins. We had the same number of formations, but we were working with about five times the number of adjustments.

During the final week of the regular season, when we were scheduled to play Seattle, I had our offensive coordinator Gary Kubiak take over and diagram what turned out to be the winning game plan for the Seahawks. I had nothing to do with it. Instead, I spent all my energies on the Dolphins and any possible rematch we might have with them.

I also studied extensive game film of the Jacksonville Jaguars and Buffalo Bills—two other possible opening-round playoff opponents—but the Dolphins got most of my energies. I went back and looked at every film of each one of their games, reviewing in detail the things that gave them the most problems. Not only did I have that extra week to prepare for them, but then, the following week, I used a good part of our bye week preparing as well.

By the time it was official we would be playing them, we had drawn up plays that we hadn't even used before. One was "Trey Dolphin right," a formation in which our backup offensive tackle Matt Lepsis was inserted as an extra blocker.

The unbalanced line helped us control Miami middle linebacker Zach Thomas and create some big holes for Terrell Davis, who rushed for 199 yards on 21 carries in just over three quarters' worth of work. The Dolphins hadn't even practiced against the formations we prepared for them. They were yelling at each other, knowing they were playing a more prepared Denver team than the one they beat up on down in Miami less a month earlier.

This preparation obsession stuff, I'm happy to report, has rubbed off not only my team, but my family. The Monday morning after our Super Bowl XXXIII win over the Falcons, I was a little late for the helicopter ride that was taking me from our hotel in Fort Lauderdale to the media center in Miami for the morning-after press conference. Now if you know me, you know I'm never late. I'm as on time as an NFL kickoff.

But when I went to get dressed that morning, my wife, Peggy, was so prepared that she had packed all my belongings the night before. And shipped them to the airport. Leaving me with no shirt for the press conference.

Rather than becoming the first coach in NFL history to imitate a Chippendale's topless dancer at a victory press conference, I wore a white Super Bowl XXXIII shirt that I purchased that morning in the lobby of our hotel. I put it underneath my sports coat and voilá—crisis averted. I was prepared for the press conference and the day ahead.

PAUL TAGLIABUE

National Football League Commissioner

As intense a game as professional football is, it's very difficult not to get caught up in it emotionally. Yet I think Mike Shanahan is a master at controlling his emotions. He is succeeding with intellect, emphasizing preparation, knowledge, planning, details as opposed to fiery pep talks and whipping his team into an emotional frenzy.

From the opportunities I've had to watch him, it has become obvious to me that Coach Shanahan is not a self-promoter, not someone who is worried about commercial endorsements or his ego. He's not dogmatic in terms of a particular system or philosophy. He is flexible, adaptable, and totally focused on preparing his team to win. This, in my opinion, is what has set him apart during the two years in which the Broncos have won back-to-back Super Bowls.

His preparation is total. It involves every aspect of his team and his players. It's not just worrying about the game plan. It's worrying about what hotel his team is staying in, what they're eating for the pregame meal, whether Bible-study sessions are set up properly, whether his team is run in a first-class manner. His preparation of the Broncos includes everything that impacts a football team.

The first time I became aware of him was during the 1980s when I was an outside attorney for the league and Mike was a highly regarded young assistant coach. He became the Raiders head coach at age thirty-five and was always in demand, whether it was the 49ers hiring him as their offensive coordinator or Broncos owner Pat Bowlen luring him back to Denver. Just from observation, you knew there were good reasons he was so highly coveted. When he became head coach of the Broncos, he certainly showed why.

Mike's accomplishments with the Broncos speak for themselves. They are especially impressive in this era of free agency when the challenge of keeping a championship team

intact is greater than ever. Mike leads by example, with confidence, and with a track record that shows he knows what it takes to win.

These are the qualities that would help anyone win, in any industry.

2

SACRIFICING
TO GET WHERE YOU NEED TO GO

The date that Peggy Brandt and I set for our wedding was February 19, 1977—national letter of intent day, when the country's top high school football players signed their names on the dotted line and agreed to attend their chosen colleges. Our thinking was, by the time the signing date rolled around, Oklahoma would be able to give me some time off.

Unfortunately, I didn't realize the school was going to have to give me permanent time off.

Late during the 1976 season, after our wedding date had been finalized, the NCAA ruled that each school had to cut back the number of part-time assistants it was employing. Oklahoma, at that time, had to get rid of four part-timers. Unfortunately, I was one. For the first time in my professional career, I found myself staring straight at unemployment.

But in December 1976, while we were in Tempe, Arizona, to play Wyoming in the Christmas Day Fiesta Bowl, Northern

Arizona football coach Joe Salem pulled aside Oklahoma football coach Barry Switzer at a party that week and asked if he had any assistants he had to let go due to the NCAA's new rule. Before Barry could answer, his wife, Kay, said, "What about Mike?"

Barry told Joe I was getting married and had to find a job. And later that week, after interviewing me, Joe offered me the running backs coaching job, although we did encounter one serious hangup. Northern Arizona was an NCAA Division I-AA school. Division I-AA schools began signing players neglected by Division I schools as of February 19th.

"Uh, Joe, that's when I'm supposed to be getting married," I explained.

"I know it's going to be tough on you, Mike, I know," he told me. "But I have to have you here. We're going to be recruiting. That's my two-week window, the only time I have to sign all my recruits. I'm going to need you based in Los Angeles."

This was obviously a problem. I needed a job, and this one, where I would learn the intricacies of the passing attack from a coach as knowledgeable as Joe Salem, was a great opportunity for me. I talked it over with my fiancée and while she understood, she naturally was none too happy. We would have to cancel our week-long honeymoon in Acapulco.

The morning after our wedding at the First Christian Church in Atlanta, Illinois—a tiny town located midway between St. Louis and Chicago—we packed up our U-Haul trailer and headed out to Flagstaff, Arizona.

Minnesota Vikings coach Dennis Green once said, "Everybody wants to go to heaven, but nobody wants to die." How true. So many times people don't realize the number of sacrifices you must make in order to have the success you want.

You don't eat fried chicken without getting a little grease on your hands. You don't change a baby's diapers without getting a whiff of something you'd rather not. That's just the way it is. So much in life is about sacrifices. We make them on a daily basis. Should we spend more time at work and lose out on family opportunities? Should we spend more time at home with our families and lose out on business opportunities? It's up to you.

If you're skipping the preparation we all need, you're not fooling anybody. That's why it's easier to just do the work—that is, if you are committed. A lot of people will just tell themselves, "Oh, forget about it." Well, really deep down, they are unwilling to pay the price. But if you are, then you never will fool yourself. You will gain confidence, and your chances to succeed will increase.

When it comes to long-term career sacrifices, my thinking always has been that you should do anything, move anywhere, outwork anyone so long as you have the chance to chase your passion and dream. Life is short, labor long.

When I first got married, I explained to Peggy the nature of the coaching profession, particularly how we might have to move more often than we'd like. I told her we would most likely move many times early on, before we had kids, but that hopefully, eventually, the moving would stop and we could settle down to a more stable family life.

She committed to this with me and it's something I've always appreciated. She has been supportive of our transient lifestyle, always packing, always moving, always acting unselfishly. But our dream was in action.

In our first four years of marriage, we lived in northern Arizona, eastern Illinois, Minnesota, and Florida, four moves in four years. At Florida we were fortunate enough to stay four more years before the Broncos offered me their wide receiver's coaching job and we moved to Denver. We stayed four years in Denver, went to Los Angeles with the Raiders for eighteen months, came back to Denver for two and a half years, went to San Francisco for three years, and then returned to Denver.

Everybody knew that was the nature of the job, but they still told me I was crazy, and that might be true. Not many spouses would have put up with this, but Peggy was always there for me. With all the changes going on around me, she was an important, beautiful constant. We made the sacrifices together, making it more bearable. Meanwhile, I was working toward my ultimate goal of becoming a head coach.

Most people, for whatever reason, think natural ability is the most important power a person possesses. It's not. People who achieve the highest level of success have an unbelievable work ethic, the desire to sacrifice.

Everybody thinks San Francisco's Jerry Rice is the best wide receiver out there. He certainly is talented, but I guarantee you he's not even close to being the most talented. He's not the strongest or the fastest. But he is the most determined.

During my three seasons in San Francisco, I remember how he used to tell me, "I want to be the best wide receiver ever to play the game." In my mind, he already was the best. He already held the all-time NFL records for receptions, receiving yards, touchdowns, games with at least 100 receiving yards, seasons with at least 1,000 receiving yards, consecutive games with a touchdown, on and on.

But Jerry's mindset was that nobody was going to work harder, prepare better, or sacrifice more. He convinced himself that he was going to outwork every receiver who came into the league relative to conditioning, lifting, studying—everything. He knew that people might not enjoy the practice, but you can't get to be the best without it.

Every day during the off-season, Jerry would be up at 6:00 A.M., going through his strenuous stretching drills. He would run seven 5-yard shuttles, which he called "stop and go's," and fourteen more 40-yard dashes up and down the field. Then he would line up fluorescent orange cones across the field and weave in and out of each one six times at full speed, working on his acceleration and cutting ability. When he finished with the cones, he would run six more 40-yard dashes, and then 20-yard patterns until he was flat-out exhausted.

Then he would lift weights in as quick a rotation as possible, no resting. Bench presses, seated bench presses, incline bench presses, power lifts, dumbbell curls with increasing weights. I get tired just writing about it. It didn't take me long to understand why every time we got to the fourth quarter of a game, while most of the players were slowing down, Jerry could run as fast as he did on the first play of the game.

On the days he trained, Jerry would cap off his physical work with mental work. He would immerse himself in game film of the league's top ten wide receivers, studying how they ran their routes and what moves they used to get open. It was amazing to me how he had so many of the all-time records, and he still was working harder than anybody.

It would have been so easy for him to be spending that time relaxing at the mall or on the golf course. But Jerry was sacrificing his leisure time to be considered the greatest wide receiver of all time. The only way was the hard way, he believed.

And eventually, even though you may think nobody notices your extra effort, somebody usually does. Your work will pay off tomorrow, a year from now, five years from now, you don't know when. But it will.

It's like Calvin Coolidge, in one of his most well-known quotes, once said: "Nothing in the world can take the place of persistence. Talent will not; nothing is more common than unsuccessful men with talent. Genius will not; unrewarded genius is almost a proverb. Education will not; the world is full of educated derelicts. Persistence and determination alone are omnipotent."

Of course, sometimes the demands of your job are going to be greater than you could ever imagine. But exceptional people don't shrink from them. They are willing to sacrifice not only for themselves, but for others.

Our running back Terrell Davis is that way. Before the first play of the second quarter in Super Bowl XXXII, when we had a 3rd-and-goal from the Packers' 1-yard line, Terrell came walking over to the sideline, unable to see anything. It was the onset of a nasty migraine headache that would prevent him from playing all but that first play of the second quarter.

"I can't see," Terrell said on our sideline, not sure who he was talking to.

"What's that?" I asked him as I wandered over to him, not wanting to believe what I was hearing.

"I can't see!"

At that time, everyone in the stadium and everyone in the country was expecting us to give the ball to Terrell. But we had looked at so much film of the Packers defense, we knew that on 3rd-and-1 from the 1-yard line, they always used an all-out blitz. Without Terrell in the game, they would be unwilling to make that total commitment to defend the run. I knew that, and I needed Terrell to know that—even if he couldn't see it.

"Okay," I told him, placing my right on hand on his left shoulder, as if everything was going to be just fine. "Just do this. You don't worry about seeing on this play because we're going to fake it to you on 'Fifteen Lead.' But if you're not in there, they won't believe we're going to run the ball, okay?"

He couldn't see, but Terrell jogged back onto the field, found his way back into the huddle, and strapped on his helmet. The play—"Fake Fifteen, Lead QB, Keep Pass Right, Fullback Slide"—was called, the ball snapped. Terrell took a fake handoff from John Elway and ran right toward the line, into the teeth of the Packers defense and linebacker Bernardo Harris. While the Packers charged at Terrell, John bootlegged into the end zone for a touchdown.

Now that's what I call sacrifice.

Of course, there are the times when no amount of work or sacrifice can turn a loss into a victory. But to give up any struggle without first giving your best can be habit-forming. And good habits come from discipline, from doing the same things over and over—one of the essential components of sacrifice.

People talk about discipline, but to me, there's discipline and there's self-discipline. Discipline is listening to people tell you what to do, where to be, how to do something. Self-discipline is knowing that you are responsible for everything that happens in your life; you are the only one who can take yourself to the desired heights.

Discipline is what we provide our players during the season. For six months, from July through January, we give them detailed schedules and game plan instructions, and expect them to carry out our orders. A perfect example is the night before a game.

After we get out of Saturday-night meetings about 9:00 or 9:15, our team still has about ninety or so minutes until our 11:00 P.M. curfew, which is strictly enforced. The majority of our players hang around the hotel, have a little snack, go back to their rooms, go over their playbooks, or just go to sleep. They understand that's the standard and sacrifice we expect from them.

Whether we are in Denver or an opposing city, I tell our team that Saturday nights are not the nights to go out drinking. If they want to do that in the off-season, I'll pay their way. I'll even keep them company if they want. But not during the season. Everything we do the night before a game is to beat the opponent.

For me, if I go out the night before a game, I feel like I take away something from my concentration, my sleep, and my team. I'm letting everyone down. Now, would it be nice to go out on the town and have a nice dinner? Sure it would. But I can't ask my players to make the sacrifice when I'm not willing to do it myself.

A lot of organizations, however, do not adhere to the same rules. Some do not require their players to stay at hotels the night before their home games. Some do not have a curfew for their team. And in my mind, they are not imposing the discipline that I believe is necessary to win.

The Chiefs did not have a curfew in recent seasons. When we were in Kansas City in November 1998 to play a Monday night game, a number of people from Denver reported to me and our players that Chiefs linebacker Derrick Thomas was sitting next to them in a restaurant at midnight. By that time, our players were fast asleep.

The next night, with John Elway on the bench, we beat the Chiefs 30–7. And in the fourth quarter, when the game got late and out of control, so did Derrick. He was penalized for three personal fouls. Who knows, maybe he was just a little grumpy from being out late the night before.

Now it would be foolish of me to suggest that having a curfew or getting to bed early ensures that you will come out on top. But it could be that getting an extra couple hours of sleep might be the fuel for the little advantage you need. Discipline does that.

Then there's self-discipline. Our players are paid their full salaries over the course of the six months of the season, but what happens when the paychecks stop coming and they are not required to be at the training complex every day? How do they handle themselves then? Are they strong enough mentally to have that self-discipline to work out on their own? That, in my mind, is what separates people.

People ask me all the time why our linebacker Bill Romanowski, a former third-round pick out of Boston College, is so good. I tell them because he prepares, he sacrifices, he has the self-discipline you wish all your coworkers did. He makes sure that outside of Jerry Rice, no one is in better shape than he. He works on getting faster, he works on getting stronger, he takes care of his body.

Bill has a plan, a daily routine. He knows what he wants to do each day of each week. He plans workouts for his chest, his shoulders, his thighs, his hamstrings, every part of his body. He has a plan for studying, spending more time analyzing the opponent during the season than any player I've ever known. He knows what he wants going into his body, he knows the nutritional supplements he takes, the food he eats, every morsel he ingests. The man is maniacal about it. He understands that you can't gain muscle eating nothing but dessert.

Bill knows the cost of care is pricey in time and dollars, but he still spends freely. Each year, it costs him hundreds of hours in personal time to train the way he likes, and an annual $100,000 for the nutritional supplements, personal masseuses, and trainers. But in my mind, Bill's intake is directly related to his output. While becoming a Pro Bowl linebacker and one of the top players in the league, Bill has not missed a single game in his eleven-year NFL career.

The guy never stops. When we were in San Francisco together, he'd be at the 49ers training facility at 10:00 P.M., taking care of his body, getting massages, sitting in the whirlpool, watching film. It's no different here in Denver. During the season, Bill is always the last player to leave our training facility, and he leaves when it's late and dark. He has the self-discipline it takes. He sacrifices some of the time he could be spending with his family. But when Sunday finally comes, no one's mind and body are more ready for the competition.

There are few people as intense as Bill. On his plane ride to Honolulu—a mere two days after we won our second straight Super Bowl—Bill turned to his wife, Julie, and in all seriousness said, "You know, I really need to start focusing on my off-season training."

To which Julie slapped him upside the head, the way Bill has done to so many quarterbacks, and scolded him. "Give it a break, Bill!" she said, exasperated. "Take a vacation!"

But on the way to success, there is little time to rest. Everyone has the same amount of time each day. It's up to you to choose how you spend it. You can sacrifice, or you can't.

The morning after our wedding at First Christian Church, our drive from Atlanta, Illinois to Flagstaff, Arizona, was more incredible than any of the travel travails Steve Martin and John Candy endured in *Planes, Trains & Automobiles.*

On the way through Springfield, Missouri, the wind was blowing so hard, we had to pull off the road into a gas station for cover. While we waited, one of the service station attendants informed us we would probably be there a while. The area was getting blasted by a tornado. I don't know that I've ever seen winds that strong in my life.

After a few hours, we were able to continue our trek, but when we got to Oklahoma City, Oklahoma, we had to stop again because we couldn't see a foot in front of us. There was as much visibility as if we had been blindfolded. Whipping through Oklahoma City was a major dust storm unlike anything I'd ever seen.

After sitting for a few hours, we continued on, though not for as long as we would have liked. Just outside of Albuquerque, New Mexico, the sleet that was falling from the sky turned to ice, freezing up the roads. Our trailer actually started coming loose. We had no choice but to pull over, reattach the U-Haul, and wait for the highway, which had been transformed into an ice skating rink, to defrost just a little.

Finally, after yet another couple-hour delay, we were off to Flagstaff, Arizona. And I'm guessing you'll find it to be no big surprise that once we arrived there, the town's biggest snowstorm of the season was waiting for us. A foot and a half of snow. We had no choice but to navigate right through it.

It wasn't *Planes, Trains & Automobiles*, but it was a tornado, a dust storm, an ice storm, and a snowstorm. And the whole time, with each of the inclement conditions we encountered, my new bride, Peggy, kept shaking her head, saying, "Just think . . . we could be in Acapulco right now."

She didn't say that to me at each stop—she said it to me the whole way out there. Yeah, we missed Acapulco—and I still haven't heard the end of it. But with all the sacrifices we made along the way, we still got where we wanted to go.

JERRY RICE

San Francisco 49ers Wide Receiver

Being the head coach or head of any company, you have to put in extra work and be willing to be the last one to leave your office if you want to be the best. By winning two Super Bowls in a row, Mike has done that.

To win that much takes a lot of discipline because you have to push yourself. It's almost like there's an inner battle going on. Your conscious is saying inside to you, "Well, you don't have to do this, you can be doing something else." But Mike knows you have to fight your way through that, and if you do, it'll pay off for you.

What's the best way to fight through it? To win that battle, you have to play games with yourself. The thing about me is that I never think about what I did the last year. I always think I can do better, and that motivates me to get out there and do that extra work to better my performances. I think any negative you always have to try to turn into a positive. You try to prove so many people wrong, and that's what Mike has and that's what I have.

The motivating factor is usually to prove wrong the people who doubt you. There were people who doubted Mike when Al Davis fired him. Getting fired does a lot to your mind because you know what you're capable of but you still have to check yourself all over again. That's what went on with Mike. He read so many negative things in the newspaper and he had to fight them off.

You don't want that to sit in your head because if you ever start doubting yourself, then you don't have a chance. That's when you're done. So you have to keep fighting and get through it and be disciplined enough to stay with your routine and believe in it.

That's one of the main reasons Mike has been successful. People focus more on Terrell Davis and Shannon Sharpe and John Elway, but they don't realize how much sacrifice it takes from the man in charge for a team to be successful.

The head coach sets the standard. He makes the job easy for his players. All we have to do is go out there and basically show our talents. But the coaches do all the preparation, they put in all the time.

It's no surprise to me he has won two Super Bowls in Denver. Mike's very, very intelligent when it comes to the game of football. You take a guy like that and throw him into an organization like Denver's, and it's just a matter of getting the players and learning the system. Mike knows exactly what to do and how to get his players to believe in him. Once he mastered that, that was basically it. That was the chemistry they needed to win two Super Bowls in a row.

But to get to that level, the sacrifices it takes are incredible. It's staying away from his family, working long hours, doing so many things people don't see, all to be the best at what he does.

3

LEARNING
TO FOLLOW THE LEADERS

To succeed, you absolutely need to gain more knowledge in your selected field. How do you go about doing that? One of the most fruitful ways is from the living lessons role models provide. It is easy to become a winner if you're simply willing to learn from those who have been winners themselves.

Find out who has had the most success at what they do. Watch their technique. Observe their methods. Study their behavior.

By going out and finding the best people in your profession, you will learn what their routines are, the mistakes they made along the way, and the various scenarios they are forced to confront on a day-to-day basis. Then not only can you imitate their habits, but you also can imitate their results. It can be that easy.

You might as well capitalize on the fact that all around you are winners willing to help enhance your talents. They are in your office and in your neighborhood, at your seminars and at your conventions. They are in so many places, so accessible, that it might actually be harder for you to avoid them than to find them.

People are very good about giving advice if only you will show that you're genuinely interested in what they have to say. They are willing to reveal what has and has not worked for them. So with little prodding, their guidance is available and their instructions can be invaluable. These are your role models. It is always best to follow the leaders.

A perfect example: In 1967, an aspiring basketball coach named Mike Jarvis attended his first coaching clinic. The man conducting it was Indiana basketball coach Bobby Knight. At the clinic, Jarvis spent $1.50 to buy Knight's book on basketball tips and to learn the finer points of man-to-man defense. Almost a quarter-century later, Jarvis was hired as St. John's basketball coach. In the 1999 NCAA college basketball tournament, St. John's played Indiana. And Jarvis wound up beating the man whose book he committed to memory.

Lessons, as inexpensive as some are, sure can come in handy.

Like Jarvis and so many other coaches, I even remember my first coaching clinic. It was back in 1974, after I lost my kidney and elected to enter the coaching profession. The clinic was the Illinois High School Association Clinic at the Hyatt Regency in Rosemont, Illinois, and when I got there, I checked the program to see the list of speakers and spotted the name Bill Walsh.

Now, Bill had not yet led the 49ers to the three Super Bowl titles he took them to in the 1980s, nor had he yet been inducted into the Pro Football Hall of Fame, as he was in 1993. But right away I could tell his lessons were good enough to last a lifetime. The lecture he delivered that day still stands out in my mind.

He said, "If you want to stay in this game, if you really want to stay in it for the long haul, learn the game better than anybody else in the profession." He urged us to know all aspects of offense, defense, special teams, every phase of the game. And then he wrapped up his talk with a lasting message. "The one thing that keeps you in the game and gives you a chance to be the best," Bill told the assembled crowd of about 1,200 coaches from around Illinois that day, "is if you know your profession inside and out."

Even then, as a twenty-two-year-old kid, that made a lot of sense to me. It has informed my career ever since.

The crucial thing about learning is that it is forever. The thrill of it never really ends. When I was growing up, I used to pay attention to all the coaches who worked with me. It was exciting to absorb the wisdom they would impart.

Of the many great coaches I encountered, the one who stood out was Jim Payne. When I was a freshman at East Leyden High School in Franklin Park, Illinois, Jim was my track coach as well as my football coach. I spent a lot of time with him. He was a serious competitor, but even more important, he was very people-oriented. He may have had a job to do, but he really cared about people, and was more than willing to spend the extra time with them. That was something that I always appreciated and always remembered.

Now, all these years later, Jim still serves as a role model for me. Nine years ago, doctors informed him he was one of 30,000 Americans with amyotrophic lateral sclerosis—Lou Gehrig's Disease. For the past seven years, Jim has been unable to speak. For the past three years, he has been unable to move. Very slowly and very painfully, the disease has been melting his nerves, destroying his body, killing my mentor and friend.

Jim has been on a twenty-four-hour respirator, but he has been a fighter. He has donated his living body to researchers at Northwestern University, so that they might be provided with some small insight into their quest for a cure against this nasty neurological disorder.

Years ago, I promised Jim that if my team ever made it to the Super Bowl, I would buy him tickets and fly him to the game. But in 1998, when the Broncos went to Super Bowl XXXII in San Diego against the Green Bay Packers and I tried to follow up on my promise, the doctors would not let Jim make the trip. It just was not possible. Jim cheered at home, in silence.

As helpless as he has been, Jim still is 100 percent mentally in control. He might have lost control of his bodily functions, but the disease, hard as it might have tried, cannot get at his mind.

Somehow, Jim has found a way to move his eyeballs enough to help move the cursor on a specially designed computer keyboard so he can write letters to his family and friends. Just as we were getting ready to play the Atlanta Falcons in Super Bowl XXXIII, Jim managed to send me a letter.

> *Dear Mike,*
>
> *You have done your usual stellar job of preparing the Broncos amidst all the hoopla of going for an undefeated season and all the other distractions that go along with being defending Super Bowl champions . . . My nurses don't bother to take my blood pressure before your games, and certainly not before the Super Bowl, as it tends to run a tad high! . . . Take care, good luck against the Falcons and please extend our congratulations to your team and staff . . .*
>
> *Best wishes,*
> *Jim Payne*
> *Schaumburg, Ill.*

The man continually amazes me. As Jim's wife of thirty-eight years, Ruth Ann Payne, remarked during the week before Super Bowl XXXIII, "How does Jim survive every day knowing that again today, just like yesterday and the day before, and the day before that, and tomorrow, and the next day, and every day after, that he can't move? How does he accept that communicating is difficult, and knowing he's totally dependent on a life-support machine in order to live, and that someone is needed to feed, bathe, shave, dress him? He can't even scratch his own nose. How does Jim do it?"

There were plenty of fundraisers for Jim, and I try to help out as much as I can financially. But the truth is, Jim helped me more than I can ever help him. Whenever we lose a game or we start feeling bad, I think of Jim—a guy who never feels sorry for himself. Jim has been a teacher. He has taught me what real strength is.

As a little boy, Joe Namath used to keep a picture of Johnny Unitas over his bed, constantly staring at the photo, using the picture as a model of what he hoped to one day grow up to be. Growing up, I would study the people who surrounded me. The lessons, applicable even today, kept pouring in.

As a child, I still remember my parents, Ed and Dorothy Shanahan, trying to instill in me the kind of work ethic I have today. When I was fourteen, my mother took me to our local library and actually forged my birth certificate to say I was sixteen so I immediately could start working and saving money.

During my high school years, aside from Jim Payne, my head football coach, Jack Leese, and his offensive coordinator, Bill Ohlson, were instrumental. They taught me the importance of unbridled commitment. They were there for their players every minute of every day. They were so determined to help other people through their coaching methods, providing them with the proper attitude they needed for life, that it couldn't help but rub off on me.

At Oklahoma, I watched the way Barry Switzer handled people. It was unbelievable. I don't care if it was whites, blacks, Indians, whomever they were, Barry knew the way to make people feel comfortable. He would go into a house on a recruiting trip, walk in there about 8:00 P.M. and not leave until three in the morning.

He didn't get caught up in his ego, thinking he was above recruiting and his assistant coaches should be doing it. He did it himself, every night he possibly could. And he did it incredibly well. It is why, in my opinion, Barry Switzer will go down as the greatest recruiter in the history of college athletics.

Barry used to have a fleet of airplanes from Oklahoma's boosters at his disposal, able to whisk recruits around in Learjets if he needed to impress them. But that was not what made him so effective. What made him so effective was his attention to detail. Before Barry went to visit a recruit, one of his assistant coaches would debrief him about what to say and what not to say. He would have a scouting report on the recruit's football skills, academic abilities, and family tree. He would be completely and thoroughly ready.

Then he would follow up with his own personal touch. I remember hearing how in 1974, the year before I arrived in Oklahoma, Barry was embroiled in a recruiting war for Billy Sims, the highly coveted running back from Hooks, Texas. But on a Saturday when Oklahoma was playing Colorado at Boulder and the Sooners led 28–0 at halftime, Barry noticed a pay phone on the wall in the visitors' locker room. He picked it up, called the service station where Billy pumped gas on the weekends, and made his top recruit feel even more important.

"We've got their ass whipped," Barry confided to Billy, who was tracking the game on the radio. "Let me tell you what we're going to run on them in the second half so you can listen for it." Billy listened to the radio and to Barry. He went to Oklahoma.

At Florida, I had the fortune of spending time around Charley Pell, the most organized person I've ever known. It didn't matter what it was, a practice, a recruiting trip, whatever—Charley was organized and ready for it. He organized the alumni in Florida from all over the state and that's why right now they just might be the most powerful alumni group in the country.

During my first year in Florida, in 1980, I found out how powerful they were. One day Charley ran into a scheduling conflict and he asked if I could fill in for him that night in Jacksonville, Florida, speaking to the Gator Club. Sure, I told him, no problem. I didn't think it would be any big deal. Then when I got there and there were about 1,400 people waiting, I couldn't believe it. Charley had organized and galvanized a big group of people who didn't have to be there.

Everywhere I went I tried to learn, assimilating the positive qualities of various employers, even if I didn't admire all their traits. I learned from Raiders owner Al Davis, the man who fired me four games into the 1989 season. When I was around him, I would ask myself, "Why has he won three Super Bowls? Why?" I knew why when I left the Raiders.

Preparation. He left no stone unturned. He knew personnel so much better than anybody else in the league, it wasn't even a contest. I could see how he did it. He used to call me at home at 11:00 P.M., when most people were sleeping, and say, "Mike, I think I can trade for this guy," or "I think I'm going to sign this guy," or "What do you think about this guy?"

He was thinking football all the time. He never let it go. He always was wondering what he could do to improve his organization. It worked for a very long time—up until some people realized what he was doing, caught him, and passed him.

Learning from experience—others' and yours—is a vital lesson of life. You may have all the book learning necessary for the highest degree. But without a degree in experience—the rough-and-tumble of life—you'll never be a full graduate. Hanging around experience and forming your own brings a quiet confidence, an inner belief that you can handle similar experiences in the future. That's why experienced people are so much in demand in our workforce. They know of what they speak.

And not only should you study their successes, but you also should study their failures. You should learn from their mistakes so you don't wind up making those same mistakes yourself. Then you have a chance to reach the level you want quicker than the people whom you are learning from.

It's also important to remember that it is not just people whom you learn from, it's organizations, the great ones especially. One of the greatest influences on me was the San Francisco 49ers organization, because I had a chance to really decipher it. With five Super Bowls in fifteen years, it might have been the greatest organization in sports at that time.

You can work and work and work, but until you find a system that's been successful over time, you might not be learning the right things. In San Francisco I learned the right things. They had a philosophy for their offense and defense, for how the organization should be run, for how the organization should draft. It was all there for anyone there to study.

It's hardly accidental that Seattle Seahawks head coach Mike Holmgren, Minnesota Vikings head coach Dennis Green, New England Patriots head coach Pete Carroll, Green Bay Packers head coach Ray Rhodes, Tennessee Titans head coach Jeff Fisher, Carolina Panthers head coach George Seifert, Cincinnati Bengals head coach Bruce Coslet, Oakland Raiders coach Jon Gruden, former Tampa Bay Buccaneers coach Sam Wyche, and I all spent time working in the San Francisco organization. It was a Hall of Fame collection of winners, a live laboratory for greatness.

At the end of the 1992 season, after my first season in San Francisco, the Broncos offered me their head coaching job. But before I gave Broncos owner Pat Bowlen an answer, I talked to the people with the 49ers first. I said, "Hey, I'd like to stay here, but I'd like to know the ins and outs on how we run the whole organization."

Being that they did not want to disrupt the continuity in their coaching staff and they liked me enough to want me to stay, they agreed. I remained in San Fransisco, and it was some of the best training I've ever gotten.

Among the numerous lessons I learned were that in order to get to the next level, the organization had to have a plan. It had to be a team. It had to be organized, focused, and prepared if it wanted to reserve its clean and well-lit place in history. There was a true commitment to excellence that became the standard. The time I spent in San Francisco taught me how things should be done in a classy, professional way.

By the time Denver knocked on my door again in January 1995, the 49ers were expecting it. One of the 49ers executives later joked with me that he tried to lock my office door to keep any secrets from escaping. I laughed and told him the materials had already been removed. They were in my hand and in my heart.

When I got to Denver, I knew what I wanted to do, yet it wasn't as if I could clone the 49ers. There still were plenty of things we had to do on our own. We took the material that we liked, added to it, subtracted from it, and found what situations work best for our team. For instance, the 49ers offense: It was so effective yet so basic. We figured we could add multiple formations to it, keep people off balance mentally, and still not affect our players' concentration. So that's what we've done.

Now that we've won two straight Super Bowls, I've got coaches on our staff in Denver who have instant credibility. Job offers are going to start pouring in. And when they leave, what do you think they're going to take with them? What they've learned in Denver. The cycle just keeps spinning around, one circle after another. What you learn from someone, someone eventually will learn from you.

One of the biggest things I've tried to do in Denver is have a role model at every position. That's how important I consider role models to be. I want them everywhere for the rest of our team to learn from. In my mind, and I believe it to be fact, we have some of the finest role models in the league.

At wide receiver, for example, we have Rod Smith and Ed McCaffrey. What better role models? They are two of the most unselfish players I've been around. They don't care how many balls they catch as long as they win.

At defensive line, Maa Tanuvasa was a player no one wanted. He was cut two different times. We picked him up, and since we signed him away from Pittsburgh's practice squad in February 1995, he has just worked and worked and worked, never said boo, and wowed everybody.

There are players all around him who have more talent, but few make more plays because Maa's in better shape and he's got a standard. Our 1997 first-round pick Trevor Pryce looked at Maa when he first entered the league and realized he was three inches taller, about ten pounds heavier, much faster and he wasn't making half the plays Maa was. It got Trevor going. It helped him become a better player.

At linebacker, nobody prepares like Bill Romanowski. John Mobley is one of the most talented guys in the NFL, but if he prepared himself in the off-season like Romanowski has, John

Mobley might be one of the best linebackers ever to play the game. These models are all around our organization, everywhere you look, there to learn from.

Most organizations also have negative role models. But believe it or not, they too can offer some of the most positive lessons. From watching them, you can learn how not to behave. I've been around coaches who have been insecure, dishonest, condescending, paranoid. That drives me crazy. Anytime I see a negative trait, and there are plenty out there, I tell myself, "Can we still win a championship with that attitude?"

A person might have ten great traits but if there are three negative ones, they bring down the person. You must make sure you do not adopt those traits, and instead use these people as positive negatives.

Now that I think about it, it reminds me a little bit of an old Arabic saying that I once came across that anyone could learn and profit from:

He who knows not, and knows not that he knows not, is a fool.
Shun him.
He who knows not, and know that he knows not, is simple.
Teach him.
He who knows, and knows not that he knows, is asleep.
Waken him.
He who knows, and knows that he knows, is wise.
Follow him.

A quarter-century ago, when I went to the Illinois High School Association Clinic, the first coaching clinic I attended, I realized how much I needed to learn. Now I have realized that once you've learned, it is your job to teach.

It is something that was on my mind during the second weekend in April, when I traveled back to my home state for the Illinois High School Association Clinic. Only this time, rather than sitting in the audience and sucking in the knowledge the guest speakers were offering, I stood on the stage, giving a speech of my own. This time I was one of the featured guest speakers.

I discussed many of the elements that have come to make up this book. And as I stood before the audience I once was a part of, my only hope was that my message stayed with them the same way Bill Walsh's stayed with me.

BILL WALSH

San Francisco 49ers General Manager

When I was doing broadcasting for NBC and Mike was coaching the Los Angeles Raiders, I'd see him often. I could tell he was unique when I met him. He wanted someone to exchange ideas and visit with. We became well acquainted over that time.

After he took the Denver head coaching job, we spent an afternoon together at my house in Woodside, California. We discussed organizational structure, exchanging ideas on the approach to the squad, organizing a format for lecturing the squad, and developing and influencing their attitude and bringing them together to bond together. All those kinds of things. Not an awful lot of technical football, just philosophical principles.

He likes to exchange information and he certainly likes to tap into other people. He has access to other highly intelligent people, and he uses it. It doesn't mean that he's going to follow their directives, but he can absorb and consume their expert ideas or testimony and then apply it where he needs it. He can certainly do things without anybody's help, but he has one of those minds where he can connect his thoughts with someone else's extremely well.

I knew that he'd be very successful. That was obvious. Now, to win the Super Bowl, you never know because there's always another team out there to play. But as it has turned out, he helped his squad come together very nicely and [John] Elway was reborn, and if you added that together during their two straight Super Bowl wins, it was tough to beat. The first Super Bowl they came in almost unexpectedly. And for their second Super Bowl, they were fully mobilized and really went right through it.

But above and beyond everything, Mike tries to learn from others, he has excellent credentials of his own, and he has that special wit and that special mind. He has a lot of inner confidence, and he is quite willing to take on big tasks and big responsibilities. That's not as much of a factor right now because of the Broncos' success, but early on, he took on that Raiders job, which was nearly impossible, and you might even say impossible.

He thought he could do that. He never really had the opportunity to find out. But that didn't stop him later. Mike's a guy who will go out and do things. And there are reasons for that. Mike's just got a keen mind, excellent intellect, he's bright, he's creative, he's well-organized. But inherently, he just has an energy and a vision, and he just knows the essence of what it takes to be successful. And the advantage Mike has now is that he's seasoned.

Mike is just an absolute natural at making decisions and commitments, implementing them and then moving on to the next challenge. He has been from the day he started coaching. He is consumed and dedicated to being the best.

4

DETAILING
SWEATING THE SMALL STUFF

One of the best-selling books of last year was Dr. Richard Carlson's *Don't Sweat the Small Stuff . . . and it's all small stuff.* In it, he sets forth his points for why you should not let the little things take over your life. "When you don't sweat the small stuff," Carlson writes, "your life won't be perfect, but you will learn to accept what life has to offer with far less resistance."

In your personal life, I couldn't agree with Dr. Carlson more. You accept little things that cannot be changed—weather, traffic, whatever—and try to change things that can.

But professionally? Sweat the small stuff. Sweat it morning, noon, and night. Make the small stuff that others might neglect a regular part of your plan. Return telephone calls promptly. Fill out expense forms neatly. Send out thank you notes for little favors. Do all the paperwork that is necessary.

With so many people having their eyes on the same prize, tending to all the little stuff easily could provide the slight edge you need. It very well could be the margin between winning and losing.

Let me give you a perfect example. After we wrap up our final practice of the week at about 10:30 A.M. on Saturday mornings, our players are free to do what they want that day until they have to report to the team hotel later that night. Most of them go back home and spend the time with their families that they might not get to spend during the week.

But before they leave our training facility, I always have the same message for them.

"Guys," I tell them. "Relax. Get off your feet today. Take it easy."

Now a lot of them might not have that chance. Their wives want them to sweep the garage, or mow the lawn, or run some errands—something. But I give each of our players an excuse not to. When their wives ask them to do housework twenty-four hours before one of our games, I advise our players to tell their spouses: "Oh, I'd like to, honey, but I can't. Coach Shanahan says I can't. Sorry."

There's nothing I can do about it, but I've got wives mad at me all the time, all over the place. But better to have them mad at me than mad at our players. Facts are facts. I don't want our players to clean up Saturday, I want them to clean up Sunday. For the most part, they have, and you better believe that the peaceful, easy feelings they're able to enjoy on Saturdays have had a little something to do with it.

With all due respect to Dr. Carlson, little things make a big difference. And as a coach making up a game plan knows just as well as an investigator trying to solve a crime, sometimes the most insignificant pieces make the whole.

Back in January, I called our local NBC-TV affiliate, KUSA-Channel 9 in Denver, and asked if they could please compose an inspirational music video similar to the one they did last year, when they put Broncos highlights to a Brian McKnight and Diana King duet, "When We Were Kings." The station told me, no problem.

The day before Super Bowl XXXIII, I walked over to Channel 9's mobile offices at our team hotel in Fort Lauderdale to see if the music video was ready. I wanted to make sure it was just right. When KUSA's weekend sports producer Roddy Babb showed me the tape, I told him it was great, but not perfect.

To me, they failed to capture a video image of each player on our team. They had the John Elway's and Terrell Davis's and Shannon Sharpe's, but I wanted them to include everyone who was a starter or backup who played any kind of significant role, even on special teams. It was a little thing, but it was an important thing, and I was sweating the small stuff.

So for the next five hours, we sat in that truck doing video edits. Roddy Babb had to take another verse of the song and add it on just to make room for all the players and all the highlights. But finally, just before dinner, the job was complete. I thanked Roddy, took the "When We Were Kings" music videotape, and showed it to our players in the team meeting the night before the game.

When we got through showing that video, our players were ready to play the Falcons right then and there, in the parking lot if that was the way it needed to be done. Of course, they had to wait until the next day. But with the adrenaline rush each player got out of seeing a video of all the work and camaraderie that had poured into the past season, they went out the next day and did a double-take.

For the second straight year, we were kings.

If you're going to do a job, you might as well do it right, down to every last detail. I remember when our wide receivers coach Mike Heimerdinger was a graduate assistant coach at Florida while I was the offensive coordinator there. One day I asked him to diagram some defensive alignments. He did, but with our dedication to things both big and little, I handed it back and told him it wasn't good enough. It wasn't that he couldn't do it, but he wasn't doing it right.

"Do it again," I asked him.

Which he did. But when he gave it to me again, I handed it back again. This time, the squares he drew were not symmetrical enough.

"Do it again," I asked him.

The third time, Mike got it right. And he has been doing it perfectly ever since.

If you want perfection, you must make it a part of your normal routine. It is the way our team approaches each workday. It's always the little things in practice that are considered most important. It's learning to strip the ball, to not jump offside, to not miss any assignments. On our team, it's something you're expected to do every minute of every day.

During practice, for example, our wide receivers must understand why I want them to break right at 10 yards on a certain play, and not 8 or 12. If they break at 8, the quarterback's not going to be ready to throw, and if they break at 12, the quarterback has to hold the ball and risk being sacked. We go through everything so the players really understand why it's so important to be in an exact place at an exact time.

There's a reason why many players now regard the Broncos as one of the preeminent organizations in all of sports. It's the small gestures we've made that have demonstrated that we care about them. I know if somebody really cares about me and is really fighting for me, I'll go through a wall for them. The same works in reverse. If somebody knows you don't care about him and aren't really fighting for him, then he won't go through the wall for you.

Me, I try to do the little bit extra for our team.

When I first got to Denver in 1995, a lot of players were skipping breakfast or, if they were eating, they were scarfing down fast food or donuts. It wasn't good for them or our team. So I began catering in eggs, cereal, rolls, fruit, and juices. We didn't charge them for it. It became a little thing that now makes the players come to our training facility a little bit earlier, spend that much more time together, and bond even more.

At lunch, most players were disappearing, driving away from our training facility for cheeseburgers or pizza. So I decided to cater in a hot lunch. Pasta, chicken, vegetables, fruit—again, no charge. Who said there's no such thing as a free lunch? Now our players spend more time bonding at the facility, more time preparing for Sunday, more time getting into the winning mindset they need to be in.

On the road trips, we make sure there are empty seats on our plane between each player. It just makes it easier on everyone. They're more comfortable, more rested for Sunday.

Once we arrive in the opposing city, each player has his own room. We don't force players to share a room with another guy. Your roommate might spend too much time on the phone or have the TV on a little too late. When John Elway was our quarterback, he couldn't sleep unless his TV was on all night. That might have been good for John, but it was terrible for his roommate.

At the hotel we stay at the night before our game, we allow each player to order two movies at no charge. It entices them to stay in the room and rest rather than go out the night before the game. The only reason I limited it to two was that some players were flipping through the channels and they might watch only five minutes of fifteen different movies. We would get hit with a $120 movie bill. Now it's two per man, and that's plenty. They appreciate it. They love it. These guys, they're making millions of dollars, and they go nuts for the two eight-dollar movies and the sixteen dollars in savings.

When we went down to Fort Lauderdale, Florida, last January for Super Bowl XXXIII, I thought it was important for our team to stay around the hotel as much as possible, to avoid the kind of distractions that Super Bowl week presents. I remember talking to our director of operations, Bill Harpole, about our options.

"What do you think we can do where these guys can have fun by staying around here?" I asked him the week before we left for Miami.

"I can get some games in there," Harpole said.

"Get as many as you can," I told him. "Whatever somebody's interested in, we'll get. We'll make this thing look like an arcade."

Well, by the time we got to our hotel in Fort Lauderdale, the second floor was cordoned off and filled with every game imaginable. Air hockey, pool tables, pop-a-shot, Ping-Pong tables, pinball machines, video games. During almost all our off-time, there constantly were thirty guys—almost half the team—in our self-made game room. And it was all free. Our guys loved it. Doing the little bit extra ensures that you're doing everything possible to make sure your organization is the best.

This spring, someone relayed to me that Julian Lennon, son of former Beatle John Lennon, said that Paul McCartney never forgets to send him a card before each Christmas and each birthday. That tells you something, maybe everything, you need to know about Paul McCartney.

Is it any great surprise he has achieved the level of success he has?

Our organization wants every i dotted, every t crossed, every q slashed. As little as possible should be left to chance. The best way to do this is with attention to structure and organization.

Look behind my desk. There's a thick set of red looseleaf binders. One binder has an itinerary for every minute of every day of this summer's training camp. Sneak a peek.

On the eighth day of training camp, starting at 8:45 A.M., we were scheduled to have a one-hour-and-forty-two-minute practice. With our players wearing pads, there were ten minutes of hitting the blocking sled, ten minutes of group drills, ten minutes of play installation, twelve minutes of one-on-one and nine-on-seven drills, ten minutes of special categories, five minutes of special teams, twenty minutes of seven-on-seven, twenty-five minutes of team drills. And at 10:27 A.M., the players were scheduled for showers, lunch, and a little extra study time for their playbooks.

That afternoon, starting at 2:45 P.M., we were scheduled for a one-hour-forty-minute practice. With our players wearing shorts, there were ten minutes of individual drills, fifteen minutes of group drills, twenty-five minutes of seven-on-seven, twenty-five minutes of team drills, ten minutes of special categories, and fifteen minutes of special teams until, at 4:25, the players were scheduled for showers, dinner, and more meetings.

At 6:50 P.M., we were scheduled for a forty-minute special teams meeting, followed by a two-hour meeting, then lights out. Time to flip the page and move on to the next day's itinerary. This is all just part of being structured. Every minute is scheduled. No moment is wasted.

In my mind, it makes for a lot of happy training campers.

During the regular season and into the off-season, I follow a similar plan. Inside my office is an eight-page calendar containing the schedule for every practice, every drill, every meal, every meeting, every off-season commitment.

I've been around organizations that won national championships and Super Bowls, and this is the way it's done. There are no shortcuts, no easy ways out. When I arrived at my first training camp as Broncos head coach—on the University of Northern Colorado campus in Greeley, about sixty miles northeast of Denver—I charted the weather to see how much rain the city gets. I wanted to compare it with the rain Denver got at that time so we could make an educated decision about where the Broncos would hold training camp once our contract with UNC ran out after the 1997 summer.

Since there turned out to be far less rain in Greeley than in Denver, not to mention the first-class way in which they treat us, we extended our contract with the school and continue to hold training camp there.

Also during that same training camp, players were surprised when we handed out two playbooks that measure up at a combined seven inches thick. The players told me, "Even God didn't have that much to say."

Now I don't set a lot of rules, but there are some details that I'm very strict about. One is punctuality. As I explained to our team, if you're one minute late, you're being disrespectful to each of your co-workers. And you're going to pay for it.

The first time a player is late, I fine him $200. The next time, $400, then $800, then $1,600, then $3,200 until finally, sooner or later, the player starts coming on time. But I do give the players a break. If they want to pay me in cash, in front of the whole team, their fines are halved. Most players don't like digging into their wallets for their tardiness. Fortunately, we have not had many transgressions. People come to understand that nobody is more important than the team, and that the simplest way to show it is to be punctual.

Another important little thing: eye contact. No matter what business you are in, look somebody in the eye when you're talking to him. In each of the past two Junes, our team has visited the White House and President Clinton. The one thing I instantly noticed about the President is that when he looks at you, he never takes his eyes off you, regardless of what's going on. When you're talking to him, you feel as though you are the only other person in the world who exists. He has that unbelievably unique ability to make you feel special.

And he didn't only do it with me. He did it with the rest of our team. After we chatted for a few minutes, I watched the way he handled himself around the rest of our players. He made everyone feel as though their presence, and what they were saying, mattered.

Now I know why he's President. The trust he can build through simple conversation is unlike anything I've ever encountered.

The last thing I'm always looking for out of people? Whether they conduct themselves like a consummate pro. A pro practices the standard, plays the standard, lives the standard.

If you solve the little problems on a daily basis, very seldom do you encounter the big problems. Big problems typically come from not addressing the little problems first. It is the reason I want to know anytime one of the people in our organization has a problem. Maybe we can help dispense the problems quickly and efficiently.

During the 1997 playoffs, our excellent nose tackle Keith Traylor was not practicing the way he normally did. He was unusually sluggish. What made it more disconcerting was this: that week we were playing his old team, the Kansas City Chiefs, in an AFC divisional playoff game that would determine who would advance to the AFC championship game. I could tell something was wrong.

I got Keith aside one day and, rather than attack him for his poor practice habits, asked what was wrong first. He revealed to me that his mother, Vernistine Traylor, was very sick. She had called him to tell him she was not doing well. So that explained Keith's abnormal behavior. I told him that if there was anything we could do as an organization, please let us know. Sure enough, there was.

The night before we left for Kansas City, Vernistine passed away at the age of forty-five. Keith didn't say anything, but we knew we had to get him back home to Malvern, Arkansas, even if it were just for a few hours. So after we landed in Kansas City on Saturday afternoon, everyone on the team but Keith was bused to our downtown hotel. Keith remained at the airport and boarded a plane we had chartered for him. He flew home alone and spent some needed time with his family. I wasn't even sure if he would return to Kansas City in time to play; under the circumstances, we told him he was under no obligation. But he did. He returned around midnight, in time to play Sunday's game.

The game was Keith's best as a pro. He had only three tackles, but he was everywhere, disturbing the peace all afternoon. At one point, Keith fell under a pile of bodies and couldn't get up. His ankle was twisted in pain, and he hobbled to our bench. But as the Chiefs took possession with 4:04 remaining in the game and began marching toward our goal line on a quest for the game-winning score, something pushed Keith back onto the field. He was one big reason we were able to turn away the Chiefs and their chances.

After the game, as our team celebrated the upset in our locker room, I stepped in and interrupted our team's party. The room grew quiet.

"Today we had a guy who played one of the best games I've ever seen a defensive tackle play," I told them. "I know his mom was watching him with a smile on her face because she had to be so proud."

Then I tossed Keith a game ball, and the team went absolutely nuts, yelling and screaming and patting him on the back. Maybe the extra steps we took for Keith were small, but they were very special to us and our team.

MATT MILLEN

Former Raiders Linebacker and Current Fox-TV Analyst

When somebody watches Terrell Davis run, they focus on him and the big hole he runs through. I couldn't care less about that. I want to see how that big hole got there. Mike Shanahan does, too. It's all the little pieces that made the big pieces easy.

Mike pays great attention to detail, taking care of the little things first. Just watch him call a game. There are very few guys in the league who get it like Mike does offensively, the way he takes advantage of what the defense is doing.

When his receivers Rod Smith, Ed McCaffrey, and Shannon Sharpe go out on pass patterns, two of the three will be used as decoys. All they'll be trying do is pull the defense out of areas, trying to influence them to go a certain way so that something opens up. It's never like, "We're going to get this guy open here." Mike doesn't call the route, for one thing. Mike's trying to figure things out. What does this middle linebacker tend to do when the tight end comes in? What does the safety do when we run a wide receiver in front of his face? All those little things. When you watch it and you study it, it's beautiful.

It's funny because if you look at him on the sideline you don't think of him as being aggressive. But he's the most aggressive play-caller in the league. Mike knows when to step on a guy's throat and when to let him up. And there's a time in every part of life and in business to do that.

And I'll tell you the biggest thing for me. I know a coach has arrived when he's not afraid to tell you what he's going to do before the game, when there are no secrets. Mike has hit that level. A lot of times you walk in to talk to head coaches and they don't want to tell you anything. It's like, "I got a secret." I mean, who cares? I can go to Mike Shanahan and say, "Why did you do this?" and he'll tell me exactly. In fact, he'll pull out his playbook before the game and say, This is what we're going to try to do.

And that's not because he once coached me with the Raiders or because we're the greatest buddies in the world. It's because he has the confidence to know what the heck he's doing. And if that wouldn't work, guess what? He'd change on the spot. That's what really impresses me. He doesn't have phenomenal players, but collectively, he has them playing extremely well together and he has his players believing he is going to get them to play extremely well together.

Mike knows that as in life, if you take care of the little things, the big things will take care of themselves. It always has been that way. Sometimes it's simple. I can name a ton of NFL head coaches who don't even know all their players. I can name you guys who are head coaches and they don't know what their defense is doing. They don't know who their nickel package defensive people are, who their dime package defensive people are, they don't know what the defense is doing. They don't know. That's very common.

But you sit down with Mike, he knows exactly what the heck is going on, and that's the way it should be. It's his team. Mike even knows the names of everyone on our TV production crew.

When I played for Mike on the Raiders, I didn't know him then like I know him now. Where I saw Mike really grow was in San Francisco. So much of coaching in today's football is believability and credibility. The players have to believe in what you're doing. So you have to have some salesman in you and definitely have to know what the heck you're talking about because guys will sniff out a fraud in a second. When you stand in front of them, you have to exude confidence, and he certainly does.

Also, he has all the skills that a good head coach, or a good manager, or a good CEO should have. It's the interpersonal skills, being able to talk to somebody, getting your point across and listening to what the guy wants, hearing not only what he's saying but also what he's not saying. The ability to see where the guy fits, not only in your X's and O's, but socially within the locker room. You have to be a salesman. You have to have a plan. You have to sell the plan.

Now in football, there are a million ways to win, but you have to settle on one and you have to sell that one. And Mike Shanahan does that better than anyone.

5

UNDERSTANDING
YOUR STRENGTHS AND WEAKNESSES

While thinking about the long road from there to here, there's one story that keeps popping into my mind. It was a turning point in my life, I now understand. Ultimately, it was a realization that other people's expectations could not set my limitations. It wasn't up to anyone but me to decide what I could or could not do.

Back when I was in the eighth grade, they held a celebrate-the-end-of-the-season banquet for the fifteen players on our basketball team at Main Junior High School in Franklin Park, Illinois. I was looking forward to sharing the evening with classmates, teachers, and parents—until our coach spoke.

He stood up in front of everyone and talked about how he believed the top ten basketball players on his team had a chance to start at the high school level and, if they worked hard enough, maybe even the college level. This was met with plenty of enthusiasm and some rousing cheers.

Coach went on to politely allude to the other five basketball players on our team—of which I was one—as a group of "try-hard guys." His impression was that we were bright young men with promising futures, but just not in athletics. He felt that our time would be better used in other extracurricular areas.

I don't know what the other four guys were thinking when Coach spoke, but I sat there a little stunned. I remember asking myself, "What do you mean I can't make it? You don't know me. I know me." Even back then, anytime somebody questioned whether I could do something, I was more determined than ever before to do it.

In whatever field you mine, in whatever number of challenges you face, it is important to keep in mind that you, more than anyone, know the powers you possess. You know your interests, your skills, your specialties. Use them, ride them, work them. They will help you reach the kind of excellence we all strive to achieve every day.

If you don't know your interests, skills, and specialties, then sit back and try to do a little self-analysis. Contemplate what it is that you do well, because everyone has some type of unique ability. Once you figure out what it is, then you can isolate your strengths and highlight them. And finding a specialty in your career, or that of somebody within your organization, can lead to huge successes.

But the first foundation of living right is seeking your true interest. If you're a painter, paint. If you're a dancer, dance. If you're a teacher, teach. But just be yourself. Nobody else is nearly as qualified. Just who are you? What are you? And, if given the choice, what would you like to do?

How many of us are in jobs that we would rather not be? Too many to count. Maybe you are even one of them. But there is only one person who can change the situation: You.

If you are unhappy in your job, try searching for the little aspects of your job that give you satisfaction. Maybe it is the money, maybe it is the travel, maybe it is the promotion awaiting you for a job well done. But try to find something to provide yourself with some inspiration to do the job the right way.

That's why it's so important to do what you love. On the day he retired from hockey in April 1999, NHL all-time great Wayne Gretzky was asked what advice he would give to the young players who have the same dreams he once had. Gretzky replied: "Play because you love it, not because you think you can make a lot of money. If you play because you love it, everything else will fall into place."

Great advice from the Great One. It is applicable to anyone in any field. Until you know yourself, until you know your strengths and your weaknesses, you will be stuck, unable to take your next step.

Have you ever considered, in an objective fashion, your strengths and weaknesses? If you are that rare individual who is perfect, then you don't need to do anything. Just drop this book and get back to doing what you were doing. But if you are like the rest of us, you'll be interested in the story that follows.

Back in the spring of 1997, *Sports Illustrated*'s NFL writer Peter King sat in my office, asking me why there was such a dearth of young quarterbacks in the league. Back and forth we went, question, answer, question, answer. Then, unexpectedly, he shifted the topic from training young quarterbacks to training young girls.

Peter was coaching the Montclair (N.J.) Orioles, a twelve-and-under girls' fast-pitch Little League softball team. They had lost thirteen of their sixteen players from the team that finished 13–6 one season earlier. His newest players were, as he described it, going to lag behind quite a bit, and he was concerned about continuing the team's success.

"Any advice you would have in dealing with a team that is likely to struggle mightily?" he asked me.

And it got me thinking back to the aging, declining, 7–9 Broncos team that I took over in 1995. I knew we were going to lag behind quite a bit. I knew the makeup of our team was not what I wanted it to be. And at that time I was concerned. The year before, the Broncos offense allowed 55 sacks—27th in the 28-team league. They lost 18 fumbles—25th in the league. They rushed for only 1,470 yards—23rd in the league. Defensively they were even worse. They allowed 396 points—26th in the league; 5,907 total yards—28th in the league; and 4,155 passing yards—dead last!

Changes had to be made. The plan we drew up and implemented—isolating two specific areas for improvement—was similar to the one that I prescribed to Peter. We wanted to improve in all areas, but the ones we concentrated on heavily were rushing offense and pass defense. In my mind, we could not win without improving drastically in those areas.

In 1996, we finished with 1,995 rushing yards—5th in the NFL—and we allowed only 3,298 passing yards—8th in the league. Since then, our rushing offense and pass defense—much like the rest of our performance—continually have improved. It's a formula I would prescribe to any group of individuals trying to improve their organization.

"Look at your team," I told Peter that day. "Look at them and figure out the two things they can do really well—as well as anybody in the league. Then make sure there's not a team in your league that does those two things any better."

Peter thanked me and, on his return flight from Denver to New Jersey, thought about the two areas where his team could excel. He knew his team's strengths and weaknesses. A strength was its infield defense, and he figured he would make it even better, to the point where it excelled. A weakness was its hitting, so he decided to turn his players into the best bunters possible. During each practice, each girl would have to attempt ten sacrifice bunts and ten bunts for hits.

By the time the Orioles' season opened, Peter still had questions about his team. But he didn't have any about its infield defense or its bunting abilities.

In the third game of the season, with Montclair playing at home against Montville (N.J.)—regarded as the best team in the league—the Orioles managed to keep the game tied until their final at bat in the bottom of the last inning. Somehow, with two outs, they loaded the bases. And up came the most inexperienced player on the team, Amy Demoreuille, a little ten-year-old, forty-two-pound, long-blonde-haired girl.

"Mr. King," the girl whispered to her coach, "I'm scared."

"Nothing to be scared about," Peter assured her. "On the first pitch, you're going to place a perfect bunt between the pitcher and first base."

She nodded, stepped into the batter's box, and did just as she was told. Amy perfectly placed the ball between the pitcher and first base, and took off running. Seconds later, the winning run scored. The Orioles players celebrated. The fans in the stands cheered. And Amy and her parents cried.

The Orioles that Peter worried so much about managed to finish their season with an identical 13–6 record to the team he coached the year before.

All because they did two things well.

They maximized their strengths.

And minimized their weaknesses.

The advice I offered Peter applies to individuals as well. An important part of my job is evaluating talent—every coach needs to know exactly what his players are capable of so they can be used in the most appropriate situations that will most benefit the team.

When I was the head coach of the Los Angeles Raiders, I knew that our running back Marcus Allen was beyond dependable. He was one of the best clutch runners in NFL history. He didn't make his living reeling off 80-yard runs; he didn't have to. He always could be counted on to deliver in short-yardage situations.

Whether it was 3rd and short, or 4th and 1, or goal to go, I wanted to give the football to Marcus. With his determination, drive, and talent, he constantly would get his team where it needed to go. For his wide array of talents, this clearly was his niche. Even when the game was on the line and everyone knew he was getting the football, Marcus couldn't be stopped.

When you're identifying your strengths, I think it's very easy to know what they are. Your strengths are the things you enjoy doing, the things you continually succeed at, the things that leave you feeling like the champion of your industry.

But it doesn't mean those talents should be left alone. They, too, should continually be worked on and improved. When it comes to strengths, I have a golden rule: You never put less time in working on your strengths than you did the year before. Self-improvement always should be the bull's-eye you're aiming at.

Right about now, it would be very easy for me to say, Okay, I've coached the top-rated offense in the NFC or AFC in each of the past seven years—three in San Francisco with the 49ers, four in Denver with the Broncos. Why do we need to go out and study what other people are doing when we're the barometer?

But you know what happens when you think that? You get eaten up alive. That's why we spent the 1999 off-season studying the NFL's top ten offensive teams, so that we can be even tougher when we try to become the first team ever to win three straight Super Bowls. We wanted to see what other offenses were doing. We wanted to see if there was anything out there that we could add to our offense to enhance any success we have already had.

Each individual and organization repeatedly are accorded the opportunity for development. It's up to you to make the most of it. Otherwise, you will suffer. Your competitors are just too smart and too hungry.

Do you think Bill Gates is not studying his competition? There's only one way a guy can be worth $80 or so billion, depending on what the stock market is at on any given day. He has to be ruthless, he has to be so damn smart that he knows not only his competitors, but himself. And the more you get to know yourself, the more you will realize that you have strengths you might not have known.

It is something that we have tried to bring out in our players, and something I believe we have successfully cultivated. Self-confidence comes from knowing your strengths, your weaknesses, and most of all yourself.

When I'm trying to motivate my team for another Sunday, I know I'm not a screamer. I treat my players the way I like to be treated myself. Mike Ditka might be yelling as loud as he can, Dan Reeves might have veins bulging out of his neck, Bill Parcells might offer up military or historical references, and there's nothing wrong with any of that. But none of that is my style.

I know that I'm not going to psych up my team for a game

with a long-winded pep talk or punching in a blackboard. I talk to them like the men they are and I do that because I don't like it when people yell at me. If you yell at me, if you demean me, then you've lost me. If you talk to me, if you give me a plan to do it the right way, then I'll go through a wall for you. It's why I am the way I am around my team. It's why everyone should know who they are and not try to act any different.

The night before we played the New York Jets in the AFC championship game, in what turned out to be our quarterback John Elway's last game in Denver, I never even raised that issue with our team. My speech was the same I would give for a preseason game or Super Bowl. It's never all that different.

The night before we played the Jets, when I talked with my team, I didn't stomp my shoes. I didn't raise my voice. I calmly delivered my message. I didn't even mention John; I didn't feel as though it were something that was necessary. To me, all our preparation, work, and game planning had been addressed during the week. We knew we were ready to play.

My last and only words were simply, "Let's go out tomorrow and have some fun."

We did. We had some fun. We won, 23–10.

Identifying and exploiting your strengths and the strengths of those around you is only part of the battle. The other is targeting your weaknesses, as well as those of your organization, and either improving them or obviating them.

You think you're the only one who has weaknesses? Everyone has them, including me. I don't compliment people nearly as much as I should, just because I expect them to do the job right every time. But what matters now is that I'm aware of the problem. And with awareness, with work and determination, strengths are sprung from weaknesses.

If you've got a problem and you don't recognize it, then you've got more than one problem. But if you do recognize it, you can minimize it and take it out of the equation.

A great example is Alex Gibbs, our offensive line coach. He is the best offensive line coach in the NFL, no question about it.

But he hates diagramming game plans; his game plans look like chicken scratches. He'd rather be out there coaching or looking at game film. So what do I say? Do I say, "No, you've got to diagram game plans?" No. I say, "Just do what you do well." I find someone else whose strength is drawing up game plans.

Some people are more preoccupied talking about other people's blemishes when they should be concentrating on their own. Do not fall into that trap. Fortunately, our team hasn't.

Back in December 1997, when we were playing back-to-back road games at Pittsburgh and San Francisco, our standout wide receiver Rod Smith dropped about five passes against the Steelers and then two more the next week against the 49ers. All of a sudden, Rod started pressing. He wanted to make a play so badly that he lost his focus and lost his concentration and lost sight of the job he was supposed to be doing. He was thinking more like this: "Oh my God, what happens if I miss this thing? People are going to boo me right out of the stadium."

We had to sit Rod down and tell him how good he is, to focus more on his strengths. Then, after practice, we had him catch an extra ninety passes each day. Pretty soon his concentration level was back. He began catching the ball with his eyes and blanking everything else out. Most important, he realized how good he was. And in the first game of our playoff run that season, against the Jacksonville Jaguars, Rod caught a key 43-yard touchdown pass from John Elway.

For the remainder of the playoffs and ever since, Rod Smith has been, just as we knew he could be, one of the league's top wide receivers.

In any business, there's a top, a bottom, and a lot of people in between. How do you pull yourself up from the bottom, out from the middle of the pack, straight up to the top? How do you separate yourself?

It's easy to know how to fall into the middle. Most people are in the middle because, in general, they are lazy. They want to go home early, they want to go party too often. They don't have a plan. They don't spend the extra hours honing their talents and skills necessary for success.

Of course, some people are happy living in a certain city or making a certain amount of money or spending more time with their family. And that's fine, I don't think there's any right or wrong ideas when it comes to what people want to do. My parents were like that. They were content living in Franklin Park, spending time at home. Nothing came before their family. They knew themselves well enough to know what was most important to them.

But you have to define what it is that you want to do. You have to be comfortable with it. And the only way to define it, and be comfortable with it, is to know yourself.

The outside world will try to bring you down. But what's outside doesn't matter. What's inside does. As Oliver Wendell Holmes once said, "What lies behind you and what lies ahead of you is of very little importance when it is compared to what lies within you."

Oh, and by the way—my junior high school basketball coach who said I would not be able to make it in high school athletics?

At East Leyden High School, with a student body population of 2,500, I was fortunate enough to be voted the athlete of the year as well as most valuable player in both football and track. Don't let anyone make you believe you can't accomplish your dream.

DEION SANDERS

Dallas Cowboys Cornerback

There are so many different things that impress me about Coach Shanahan, but first and foremost is this: There are a lot of coaches out there who have horses, but what they do is they put a buggy on them. And Coach Shanahan doesn't do that. He uses a horse to be a horse.

He doesn't use a horse to carry a buggy. He doesn't use a horse to plow a field. He doesn't use a horse for any of that stupid mess. He uses a horse for a horse. And it's just beautiful the way he does it.

Just for example, take a guy like wide receiver Eddie McCaffrey. Eddie has great talent, but Mike has taken him to another level. That's what Mike does. He puts his players in the right position. He knows their strengths, and their weaknesses also, and he utilizes them.

Coach Shanahan has tremendous vision. When we were together with the 49ers, I saw him diagram plays in practice and state what the safety would do, what the linebacker would do, what the linemen would do, and it all came to pass. He would say, "This guy's going to do this, this guy's going to bite, just give him this move and okay, it's going to be a touchdown." And boom! Much to our amazement, we watched what he had already produced.

He's very intelligent, but because of all the weapons he has, he doesn't get the credit he deserves. People take him for granted. I mean, there are some people who actually believe that if he didn't have a Shannon Sharpe and a Terrell Davis or some of those other guys, he wouldn't be as successful a coach as he is. That's not true. Those guys were there before he got there, and what did the Broncos do then?

He knows how to attack strengths and weaknesses about as well as anyone I've ever seen. I would hate to see him in a boxing ring because I'm sure it wouldn't take him long to figure out how to take me out of there. But he knows just what to do with everybody he has. He's like a good chess player, so graceful and so great at the game that he controls.

During our time together in San Francisco, when we were both with the 49ers in 1994, I just witnessed a magician at work, a master at his trade. Even this season, when the Cowboys came to Denver and they put up 35 first-half points against us, I went over to [defensive end] Neil Smith after the game and told him, "You guys are going back to the Bowl." I knew.

We were supposed to be a pretty good defense and a pretty good team and he just picked us apart in a manner that was mind boggling. I said, "How can a man dissect our whole defense the way he did?" It was unbelievable. And all week long, I had told our defensive coaches, "I'm telling you, the man is an offensive genius. He is." And we got back on the bus after the game and I didn't have to say it. I just looked at them. They didn't want to hear it from me. But I gave them this nod like, "Did I tell you?"

But you know what is really brilliant to me? The way he thinks ahead. When Denver played Miami on that *Monday Night Football* game [in December 1998], I said, "Now watch this master at work." Most people would have an ego and go out there and just try to run up and down the field on the Dolphins and prove themselves. I said, "'Being that he already has the division and home field advantage locked up and put away, he's going to let them play their hand like a great poker player."

Coach Shanahan knew he was going to see them again somewhere down the line, and he let them play their hand. They showed all their cards. He said, "You can have that Monday night game if it means so much to you, I'll take the playoff game." And that's what he did to them. Playoff time came around, and the Dolphins and Broncos met again, and Coach Shanahan launched his arsenal. It was good night, Dolphins.

Then I watched the Super Bowl and he used one of the same game plans he attacked us with. He came out with the five wide receivers. But when I knew the game with Atlanta was over was on the third play of the game. Atlanta came out in a certain set and they ran the ball on the first two downs and were successful. Then they went to another set on 3rd down and Denver's defense backed off and already knew it was pass. I said, "This game is over. Denver's got them finished already. They will never figure out Coach Shanahan's tendencies. Never, never." I don't know if anyone can.

Just seeing the way he approaches the game is truly a blessing for me. The calmness, the coolness, the not cracking under pressure, the never getting too far up or too far down. He is always on an even keel. And once he unleashes his horses, it's lights out.

6

SETTING GOALS
THE MILESTONES TO YOUR DREAMS

Each night before work, I pull out a piece of paper and make lists. Neatly, I script the tasks that need to be performed the next day. I put the tasks in writing so I can review them, update them, revise them, stare at them, and ingrain them into my thinking.

These are my short-term goals. And this is how I go about attaining them: list them, do them, check them off.

For instance, on the sunny March day I wrote this chapter, my list was long. It included my main goals of trying to renegotiate the contracts of defensive tackle Keith Traylor, defensive end Neil Smith, wide receiver Ed McCaffrey, center Tom Nalen, and linebacker Bill Romanowski to try to give our team more flexibility under the salary cap. I planned to meet about the party in early June at the Broadmoor Hotel in Colorado Springs, during which we were present our players with their Super Bowl XXXIII rings. I planned to huddle with our scouting department to go over the April NFL draft.

Those were my goals for that particular day. The next day they were different, but their importance was not. Establishing goals is critical. Goals are the detailed road maps to your dreams. If you don't have goals providing the direction, how in the world are you going to find your way there?

But if you have a plan, and if you have your direction laid out, you can chart your progress to your dreams at each stop along the way. And just as important, all along the way, you can see how far you've come.

It's something I've done ever since I became a coach at the University of Oklahoma back in 1975, after I realized I was not as organized as I had hoped to be. I would get home at the end of the day and say, "How could I forget to do this and that?" So I started writing things down, making a checklist. And since then, I've found it to be the most efficient way to attack the day.

Now, when you get to work, instead of going to get a cup of coffee or playing on the Internet and making small talk with your co-workers, you do something else. You think, "What do I need to get done today? What's on my list?"

If I don't have my list, I might want to go work out for an extra hour or take an extra hour for lunch or go hit a bucket of golf balls at the driving range. But if I know I have something I have to do, something that is written down, it's much easier to get it done.

A lot of times, the things on the list might even take you less time than you thought. If you jump right into them, you might be done in three or four hours. Then you have freed up bonus time to accomplish other valuable tasks or to get ahead at work.

The moment you start moving toward a reachable goal, then you start becoming successful. It is the reason you must constantly create challenges for yourself. Then, once you reach them, set some more. Push the bar higher. Your life will take on a direction it might not have had before. Impossible dreams will start to seem possible. All because of the simple goals you planned, listed, did, and checked off.

Your words and wishes can come to life.

• • •

Goals are something I demand not only of myself but of my team. Right before each season kicks off, we ask our players to submit a list of their individual goals to their position coaches. Our team's collective goal is, without question, the same: Winning the Super Bowl.

But everyone also has their own individual goals, and we have them list them so that we know, and they know, exactly what they're aiming at.

During my first season as San Francisco's offensive coordinator in 1992, I sat down and talked with 49ers quarterback Steve Young about the goals he wanted to achieve in the coming seasons. Steve was in a situation where he had failed in Tampa Bay, and then, after he arrived in San Francisco in 1987, he had spent the next five seasons playing behind Joe Montana. For a while, Steve became San Francisco's stepchild. There were plenty of people who doubted him.

In 1992, while Joe still was recovering from his elbow surgery, Steve knew his chance was finally coming. When we talked, he told me he wanted to be the NFL MVP, and go to the Pro Bowl, and win the Super Bowl. Now, not many people would have given him much of a chance. But I didn't think Steve was being unrealistic. He worked so hard in the off-season, and studied so much film, he was giving himself every chance to do it.

Of course, there were times when he wondered whether all the work would be worth it. There will be times when you wonder the same. Sometimes you're going to say, "Damn, I'm in over my head." You would not be alone in feeling that. But if you spend the time researching and preparing, if you know what it takes to fill that position, if you push yourself to work hard, then the odds will be in your favor.

You'll start telling yourself, "I deserve this." And you will start achieving your short- and long-term goals, as Steve did.

In 1992, he failed to achieve his ultimate goal, but he did lead the 49ers to a 15–3 record, and he did get selected to the Pro Bowl and he did win the NFL's MVP. In 1993, he went back to the Pro Bowl, but still no Super Bowl. In 1994, my final season with the 49ers, Steve achieved the trifecta. Again, he was a Pro Bowl selection, and again he won the league's MVP award after setting an NFL single season record with a 112.8 quarterback rating. But most important, after two straight seasons of losses to the Dallas Cowboys in the NFC Championship game, Steve got to the big game and won the Super Bowl.

Not only did he win it, he was also the Super Bowl XXIX MVP for throwing six touchdown passes in the game—a record I don't think will ever be broken.

Reaching his goals was an amazing experience for Steve. But it did take its toll. That night, just as he got in the limousine to take him back to our team hotel, he felt lightheaded. He felt like he might pass out. He felt his stomach turning worse than it did before the start of the game. Suddenly, Steve could not help himself. He leaned over and threw up. All over his agent's shoes. Then it was back to work.

Once you achieve each of your major goals, like Steve did, it's time to set more. There is always room for improvement. And the more valuable the goal, the more effort it demands.

In December 1919, when Walt Disney grew tired of his job sorting and delivering Christmas mail for the Kansas City Post Office, he and his friend formed a film company named Iwerks-Disney Commercial Artists. By 1922, Disney had created a series of Laugh-O-Gram films to be shown at Kansas City's Newman Theater, including *Little Red Riding Hood, Jack and the Beanstalk,* and *Puss in Boots.*

Did they stop there and call off their production? Hardly. Those film house vignettes were the beginning of today's multi-billion-dollar industry for youth and family entertainment.

For myself, I've always had a goal that when I turned fifty-five, I wanted to be financially secure enough that I never had to coach again. I see so many people in the football and business worlds who get to be fifty-five and don't want to be working anymore, but have to. They have no choice. They lack the funds needed to retire. If I could, I wanted to avoid that.

So from the time I started cashing my first paychecks, I was saving whatever I could. Some months, it was only $50. Others it was $200. But I constantly was asking myself, "How much do I have to save every two weeks to be able to retire at the age of fifty-five? How do I want to disburse my money? Stocks? Bonds? Real estate?" I designed a financial game plan that was intended to take care of me and my family in the future, for emergencies, the unexpected, and retirement.

If I stopped working today, I could tell you how much money I would need to live on. I could tell you relative to the money I have saved where I could live, and how much I could spend and still be able to maintain the lifestyle to which I and my family are accustomed.

Sadly, most people have no idea what it would take to live on six years from now if they retired today. Some people just wait a little too long to draw up their game plan. It's never too late, but the earlier you start, the better off you are.

It shouldn't be a complicated plan; in fact, it should be rather easy. Save your money in whatever manner you feel most comfortable—stocks, bonds, CDs, mutual funds, even your mattress. Ask advice, do research. Money is a reality that will never vanish. Treat it seriously.

Limits are self-imposed. But there are no limits to human energy, nor the goals you can achieve. A tireless effort is the most dependable way to succeed. You've got to keep going, day and night, night and day, and keep your eye on the goal.

Take something as simple as exercise, for instance. Without an incentive, a lot of times I'll wind up skipping my workout. But if I know what I want to do, I feel like no one can get in my way except myself.

In 1985, I set out to run my first marathon. I built up to it, first running five miles, then ten, then fifteen, until eventually I could run all twenty-six. And I did it in three hours and thirty-five minutes. The next year I did a 10K. My goal was to break forty minutes and I did it—just barely, but I did it. In my book, just barely's don't count if you lose—only if you win.

In 1997, I set out to bench-press 275 pounds on free weights. Weighing 175 pounds myself and not lifting a lot, I had to figure out a way to motivate myself. Every day I had a plan to build up the weight from the 175 pounds I was lifting, until one day at the end of the football season I got to the magical, and initially seemingly impossible, 275. The loftier your goals, the greater your potential.

My newest goal, which I have been chasing since the 1997 season, is beating our owner Pat Bowlen in the bet we have. He says he can bench-press 175 pounds—his own weight—ten times before I'll be able to run a mile on the treadmill in under five minutes. We bet $2,000.

Since then, Pat has spent a lot of his free time in the weight room and I've spent the little free time I've had pounding Denver's streets. For a while, it looked like Pat had pulled in front, nearing the finish line as the clear-cut winner. But then, as friendly as we are, I figured I'd dupe him. When he was getting close to his bench press, I told him to widen his grip a little bit, it would help him. By doing that, his shoulders got really sore. It was at the point where he couldn't lift for about two weeks, and he accused me of using some unfair tactics.

I can't help it—I just love to win.

I know it's going to be harder for me to run the five-minute mile because my hamstrings are getting tighter and tighter. But that's fine. I have a good goal, one that's making me run. I know I have to run every day, work more on my flexibility, work more on my leg strength. No matter if I do it or not, I have helped myself physically. That, ultimately, is the goal.

Meanwhile, Pat and I are still going at it every day. And to be honest with you, I hope we both make it. But I'm smart enough to know that if I make it and he doesn't, and I'm happy and my boss isn't, then who really wins?

Focusing on your goal sometimes allows you to bypass some of the obstacles that inevitably will pop up and try to block your path. But sometimes you will be blocked. It happens to everyone.

That's life. There are going to be times you fail to accomplish your goals. There are going to be setbacks. How do you deal with them? Are you persistent? Are you driven? Are you hungry to achieve them?

So often when the road gets a little tough, people back off, thinking they can't accomplish what they set out to do. But do not interpret temporary setbacks as failure and allow it to frustrate you. Stick to your plan. Continue focusing on your goals. Certain short-range goals will not be achieved, but the long-range goals will help keep you from growing frustrated.

How easy would it have been for our standout wide receiver, Ed McCaffrey, to quit when he was stopped short of his goals? Very.

During July 1994, the New York Giants cut Ed, sending him the direct message he couldn't play in the league. Ed was devastated. But his dream was to start in the NFL. He joined me in San Francisco in 1994, then in Denver in 1995, but didn't start either year. In San Francisco, Ed couldn't beat out Jerry Rice or John Taylor. In Denver, he couldn't beat out Anthony Miller or Mike Pritchard.

But in 1996, through hard work and persistence, Ed made it. He started 15 games and caught 48 passes for 553 yards and 7 touchdowns. Once he started, he reassessed his goals. Correspondingly, his performance got only better. During December of the 1998 season, Ed was selected as the AFC's number one Pro Bowl receiver.

All along, Ed saw his situation in 3D: He had desire, determination and dedication. In the end, he did more than they thought he could do. And now, after a season in which he caught a career-high 64 passes for a career-high 1,053 yards and a career-high 10 touchdowns, he still is not satisfied. He is determined to have another career year to top it.

And while we're on the topic, there's one other point that's pertinent to remember about coming up short on your goals: There's no need to seek gold the first time and every time out. Football is a perfect example. You can't score on every play. No one can, not Terrell Davis or anyone else. It's just not possible.

But you can turn yards into first downs. And you can turn first downs into touchdowns. And even though you haven't scored on every play, you've scored enough to achieve a universal goal.

Winning.

Right about the time I was ten, my father asked me, as most fathers ask their children, "What do you want to be when you get older?" And I told him, like I'm telling you, "I want to be a coach."

So from very early on, I had a goal, a clear and well-defined goal.

As a kid I was thinking if things worked out all right, maybe I could be a high school head coach in Illinois. Then when I got to Eastern Illinois, I figured maybe I could be a head coach for a Division II school. Then when I went to Oklahoma, I figured I could be a college head coach on the Division I level. Until my first NFL job in 1984, when Dan Reeves hired me as the receivers coach of the Denver Broncos, my goal never was to be a head coach in the NFL. Until then, the thought never entered my mind, not once.

In 1988, I got my first chance with Al Davis and the Raiders, although it did not turn out to be the chance I thought it would. The chance that turned out to be real and authentic, the chance I'm most appreciative of, came in January 1995, when Denver owner Pat Bowlen hired me right about the time Steve Young's agent was cleaning off his shoes.

Even though Philadelphia and Seattle were interested in talking with me about their coaching vacancies, Pat was determined to get what he wanted and hire me as the Broncos next coach. The way he had it planned, nothing was going to stop him.

Hours after the 49ers beat the Chargers in Super Bowl XXIX, Pat trolled through the lobby of the Miami Airport Hilton wearing a baseball cap pulled down to shield his face. No one recognized him, not even Gary Kubiak, the former Broncos quarterback then serving as the 49ers quarterbacks coach, whom Pat walked right past. Pat made his way up to my room, entered it, and handed me his contract proposal, and after two hours of discussing the deal, we reached an agreement.

His complete confidence in his ability to get me to accept his job offer was inspiring. He felt I was the best man for the job, which was flattering, of course, but that hotel visit proved he had desire and would stop at nothing to win. His goal of hiring me met my goal of being a head coach.

Two nights later, as I stood in front of an auditorium full of reporters and cameras and team officials, I reintroduced myself to Colorado.

"I'm used to winning and I like winning," I said in one of my first comments at the press conference to announce my coaching appointment. "Do I think we can win? Yes, we're going to win. Do I think we're Super Bowl caliber right now? No. Can we get there? That's my goal."

So even from my first day in Denver, I was thinking about setting goals and reaching them. But that's the way it is. Long-term success stems from short-term success.

You now have a choice. It's a simple one. You can suffer through the long hours of practice it takes to achieve each of your daily goals, or you can suffer through the extreme disappointment you will interminably feel for not knowing the joy associated with achieving your dreams. It's up to you.

As you strive to reach your goals, remember that pain is temporary. Pride is forever.

JOHN ELWAY

Former Denver Broncos Quarterback

As I said at the press conference at which I announced my retirement, Mike is the absolute best at winning football games. Thank God I got a chance to play for him before I was done. He made me the player I am. I couldn't have done it without him.

I might not be around anymore, but as long as Mike is, the Denver Broncos are going to be just fine.

That's because Mike is highly motivated to be the best coach out there. He's almost obsessed about it. And lately, I think his motivation comes from two bad experiences. One was the relationship he had with [Raiders owner] Al Davis, and the other he had with [former Broncos coach] Dan [Reeves].

The one with Al didn't work out, and I think that shocked him and made him even more determined to be the best coach out there. The one with Dan sent him into high-warp speed about wanting to be the best. Together, those two guys put this man into overdrive.

A lot of times, time heals those feelings. But I think Mike got hurt bad enough to where I don't think he'll get over it. It has fueled him to want to be the best coach ever, and the better he does, the more he can rub their faces in it. Those are Mike's goals. That's what he wants to do.

I laughed at him two, three years ago. I asked him, "Mike, what's your goal?"

He said, "Well, to be financially secure."

I said, "C'mon, you're talking to me now, not somebody who doesn't know you. Don't give me that. You know that you're always going to have a job and you know you're going to be financially secure, so don't even try to tell me that. What's your goal?"

Then he told me, "I just want to win the first game of the season."

I was like, "*Oooookay*, here we go."

He never 'fessed up, and he never told me, but he wants to be the best and make everyone who thought he couldn't miserable. But I know him better than anybody else knows him just because of the amount of time we've spent around each other. I know the way he thinks.

If he gets a chance, he's going to absolutely bury you. And that's his personality, full-speed ahead, 100 percent. He does a good job coaching because the pressure is always on himself and everyone around him. The way I explain his philosophy is like this: You're in a swimming pool and Mike always has got his foot on your head. You're struggling to get air, he's keeping that pressure on top of your head, and it's tough to keep your head above water before you sink. Then he'll go ahead and push a little bit harder and get you underneath but then, right when you think you can't go any farther, he'll let up and let you get a breath. But then, here comes the pressure again. It's a fine line of keeping the pressure on and knowing when to let up, but he knows it.

With a lot of coaches, when you win they pat you on the back. There's not a whole lot of patting with Mike. He's a classic grinder. Classic. He never lets up. His thumb just pushes on you harder and harder when you win. When you lose, surprisingly enough, he pulls it back. But when you win, there's no letup.

It's absolutely amazing to me that considering what Mike has done the last two years, he's gotten very little recognition. He hasn't won Coach of the Year once, and how can that be? You look at Dan Reeves getting Coach of the Year and then you think of what Mike has done in his first four years in Denver and the attention he has gotten for winning two Super Bowls. Not as much. Not nearly as much. Eventually that will change, but it hasn't yet.

In the meantime, Mike will not let anything get in his way. Football is his number one priority, and there are no ifs, ands, or buts about that. Nothing will get in the way of him doing his job and meeting his goals.

It's his drive to be that great, and he is. He's the best.

7

BELIEVING

SUCCESS COMES IN CANS, NOT IN CANNOTS

In life, winning breeds winning. The more you do it, the more you expect to do it, and the more you believe you can do it. It informs and brightens your attitude, making you more positive and, consequently, nearly impossible to beat.

Our Broncos team has had it instilled into it from the preseason to the regular season into the postseason and through the off-season. Its record the past three seasons speaks for itself: an all-time NFL best 46–10, including playoffs and Super Bowls.

Every time we step on the football field to conduct business, our attitude is not to simply beat the competition. It is to dominate them.

And if we are as physically strong as we are trained to be, and if we are as mentally tough as we are drilled to be, this type of attitude is only natural. Our opponents can sense our confidence, our belief that we are unbeatable, and it makes them feel that they will be in for a serious battle. They will be watching us, thinking, "These guys are executing, they're producing, they're believing, they're doing all the right things, they're performing better than we ever thought they could. How in the world can we beat them?"

Once you get your competitors worried, once you let the seed of doubt creep in and sprout up, the battle is half won. They begin to have doubts, to think about you rather than concentrate on themselves and their game. Their confidence undermined, the doubts become a self-fulfilling prophecy.

Attitude cuts both ways—and you can use it to your advantage.

Work on forming the best possible attitude of any person you know. Be more positive than any of your friends, family, or co-workers. It has been one of the biggest assets for the NFL's Most Valuable Player, our running back Terrell Davis. Once, when he was asked to sign his autograph on an eight-by–ten glossy picture of him flexing his biceps like Popeye, Terrell lifted the black magic marker to it and scribbled, "You have the strength to overcome any obstacle."

With a positive attitude, there is nothing you can't do.

What you believe, you can achieve.

My first season in San Francisco, the Dallas Cowboys upset us in the NFC championship game, 30–20. My second season in San Francisco, the Cowboys beat us once again in the NFC championship game, 38–21. Going into my third season in San Francisco, the pressure on our organization multiplied to enormous proportions. It was the season in which we were supposed to go back to the Super Bowl and back to glory.

In an effort to catch and overtake the defending champion Cowboys, the 49ers spent the off-season bolstering their roster as much as any team had in this free agency era. They signed linebackers Rickey Jackson, Gary Plummer, and Ken Norton Jr., and cornerbacks Toi Cook and Deion Sanders. Anything less than a Super Bowl win was unacceptable.

Yet in the fifth game of the season, when we were playing

Philadelphia in San Francisco, the Eagles blew us out 40–8. Now, it didn't matter that our record still was a better-than–.500 3–2. It didn't matter that we had all kinds of injuries along our offensive line. All that mattered was that our fans were furious.

As my family and I drove home from the loss that night, one of the sports-talk radio shows conducted a poll about which 49ers coaches should be fired first. With my children listening, they asked how many people thought our defensive coordinator Ray Rhodes (now the Green Bay Packers head coach) should be fired. The responses came back at 50 percent.

They then asked how many thought offensive coordinator Mike Shanahan should be fired. The responses came back at 76 percent.

They then asked how many thought our head coach George Seifert (the man who succeeded Bill Walsh in 1989 and is now the Carolina Panthers head coach) should be fired. The responses came back at 80 percent.

The next morning, our coaches thought the mood at the 49ers training facility would be tense and uneasy. But George arrived as upbeat as a beaten-down man could be.

"Men," he told his assistant coaches in our morning meeting, "I believe in our system. I believe in you. I believe in what you've done. Now's the time to get this thing straightened out."

After he addressed us, he moved on to the more difficult task of facing the press. One of the first questions involved the exact talk that my family and I had heard on the radio the night before. The reporter asked if George had heard about the poll in which 80 percent of the people in the San Francisco area thought he should be fired.

"I have," George replied.

And? What do you have to say about that?

"Well," George said, "I would like to thank the twenty percent of the people who voted for me."

Now that's what I call a positive attitude.

From that point on, the only game we lost the rest of the year was our regular-season finale, after we had clinched the NFC West title and home field advantage throughout the playoffs and we had pulled our starters from the game before the second quarter. We didn't just beat our opponents. We dominated them. In our thirteen season-ending wins, our average margin of victory was more than 20 points per game.

And after we dethroned the Cowboys in the NFC Championship game 38–28 and beat the Chargers in Super Bowl XXIX 49–26, not many people were calling for George, or anyone else, to be fired anymore.

So much has to do with what you set out to do, and your state of mind. It doesn't matter who's the smartest or the shrewdest, the biggest or the strongest. If you think you can or can't, then you're probably right.

During the 1998 season, it could have been very easy for our team to get down on itself. Our leader, quarterback John Elway, was forced to miss four starts due to hamstring, back, and rib injuries. We had not won a game John failed to start since 1989. With our quarterback sidelined, we had a built-in excuse for not winning.

But people don't care how turbulent the air is, they just want you to land the plane. So we asked Bubby Brister to replace John and to try help land our plane. We didn't make Bubby feel like he was filling in for sidelined greatness. We made him feel like he was our man, which he was.

Bubby came in and played exceptionally well. In order for that to happen, Bubby had to be ready, everybody had to be on top of their game, and we had to maintain the belief that it didn't matter who was in there, we were going to win the game.

Before the 1998 season, everybody said, "Hey, if John retires, the Broncos don't have a chance, right?" Then Bubby came in and played well. Attitudes shifted. The plane landed safe and sound. In the four games John failed to start, the Denver Broncos were 4–0. As great a player as John was, and as much as he meant to our organization, I'm optimistic we can have similar success without him. More importantly, our team believes this, too.

Of course, building a positive attitude and maintaining it can be tough, particularly with all the negative people there are in this world. So many people in so many organizations are so unhappy with their lots in life, they'd almost be better off in anger management classes. They just love to bitch. They thrive on it. I refer to this unhappy lot of people as bitchers.

They complain about their jobs, about their spouses, about anything and everything, as if they have a monopoly on misery. As if others really want to hear it. They don't, but bitchers in the fraternity of the forlorn don't care. They try to drag you into their miserable little cave dwellings, where success never will pay a visit.

In our organization, if the bitchers have a complaint about our team or their treatment, I want them to see me and tell me what's on their mind. I want to hear their problems so that I can solve them before the situation gets any worse. If you're a bitcher and you're telling your teammate that you don't like a coach, or you don't like the way we practice, or you don't like the way we run our organization, and you don't come see me first, then your negative attitude will fester and possibly spread.

And then you are a problem-maker, not a problem-solver. That is something we cannot allow. If you have any hopes of pushing your organization to the next level, you need fewer problems and more problem-solvers.

Even some of the top players complain every now and then. Former Broncos Pro Bowl wide receiver Anthony Miller, whom I coached for two seasons in Denver, felt he didn't get enough balls thrown to him during the games. To me, this was a selfish request that could have been detrimental to the team. What matters is winning, not your stat sheet. It's one of the reasons we released Anthony before the 1997 season in which we went on to win the Super Bowl.

The flip side of this is Anthony Miller's replacement, Rod Smith. When we beat the Green Bay Packers in Super Bowl XXXII in January 1998, Rod did not have any balls thrown his way. He did not catch a single pass. A lot of people told him, "God, why didn't you get the ball? You were in the Super Bowl and you were a starter and you didn't even touch it? Aren't you disappointed?"

This is how disappointed Rod Smith was. After the game was over, he was doing cartwheels on the Qualcomm Stadium field, celebrating the Broncos' first-ever Super Bowl victory.

That's what I call a winning attitude.

Back in the late 1980s, the Broncos had a cornerback with poor practice habits. Watching him practice one-on-one drills was something I will not soon forget. During the drills—with wide receivers running patterns one-on-one against cornerbacks—he wouldn't even move. He wouldn't do anything. He would just stand there.

The defensive coordinator or defensive backs coach might challenge him every now and then, but Dan Reeves, who was the Broncos coach at the time, wouldn't say anything. He wouldn't chew him out. Dan just watched him loaf. Problem was, so did everyone else on the team. Soon enough, other players were saying, "Well, wait a minute. If he doesn't have to practice hard, then why do I?"

Eventually the lack of work ethic can seep into an organization and destroy it. No one, no matter how important a person is to an organization, is above hard work. And every coach or manager has to reward or punish his people as appropriate.

I wish I could say I've never suffered from having a negative attitude. But I can't. Probably the worst time was in 1988-89, when I was head coach of the Los Angeles Raiders. I couldn't get along with the Raiders' owner, Al Davis. He insisted things be done according to his plan, not mine. He wasn't interested in my input. It was a terrible environment to work in.

Two of our coaches, Alex Gibbs and Pete Rodriguez, used to jog together and try to vent their frustrations. While running, they had a little joke.

"Pete," Alex would say, sighing. "We've got the greatest job in the world except for two things."

"And what would those be?" Rodriguez would ask.

"Earthquakes and Al Davis," Alex would say. "But at least we can live with the earthquakes."

That gives you an idea of how dreary the mood was. Things were so bleak that it became difficult to remain positive. This was so different from the other supportive, interactive environments I had worked in up until then. With my coaching reputation at stake, I struggled to stay upbeat, but the players could feel the negative vibes running through the organization.

We went from a 7–9 record in 1988 to a 1–3 start in 1989, when Al fired me. It left me dejected, but it also left me with a realization: Things don't always go perfectly. The course of human events rarely goes according to one's plans. You're going to be down sometimes. Everyone is. But that's when it's most important to keep the faith, to rely on the optimism that you must make your foundation.

Hey, our team could have gotten down in the January 1999 AFC championship game against the New York Jets. Early in the third quarter, they were beating us 10–0. I can't even tell you the last time the Broncos had been shut out at home during the first half. Everything was going the Jets' way. It looked as though on the 30th anniversary of their only Super Bowl win, they would be going back to Miami, where the Jets upset the Baltimore Colts in Super Bowl III.

But at halftime, our team did not grow discouraged. And our veteran quarterback, John Elway, stood up in front of the team and delivered the message that everyone should be thinking whenever they get down.

John told our team that we were not where we thought we would be at that point, we had made enough mistakes, we had enough chances, now it was time for us to start taking advantage of them. Now it was time to get it done. John's meaning was clear: It was winning time.

If we had allowed ourselves to quit working hard and to give up, we obviously would have been doomed. But we refused to look back at the failure of the first half and instead looked forward to the opportunity to win in the second half.

We came out in the second half and wasted little time. Three minutes into the third quarter, on a 1st-and-10 from our 36-yard line, John launched a 47-yard rocket that wide receiver Ed McCaffrey reeled in. The momentum shifted. We went on to score the game's next twenty-three points, beating the Jets for the AFC championship.

If these anecdotes prove anything, it's that life can be a wonderful adventure once you change your perspective on it. Instead of confronting challenges with gloom and trepidation, attack them with enthusiasm and confidence. Then you'll wake up every day feeling good—about yourself and about life.

This isn't to say that gaining self-esteem, self-confidence, and a sensible amount of self-satisfaction comes easy. Like life, it is difficult. You have to work at it. But it essentially comes down to acknowledging three things: 1) you are as good as anyone else; 2) if you are willing to devote the necessary time and effort to a task, success is likely; and 3) there's no reason you can't be as happy as you choose to be.

In my mind, there's no question that a positive attitude is closely correlated with self-esteem. When you feel good about yourself, you will be more upbeat, and vice versa. I have not quite been able to figure out which comes first, but it's clear you can't have one without the other.

It is up to you to find out what makes you feel great. Maybe it's dressing to the nines. Maybe it's working out, getting in a good walk or run every day. Doctors already have proven that intense workouts head off osteoporosis and depression and build self-esteem. The whole mind-body connection, without question, is there.

With me, I love exercising. I love to run and lift. It's something I try to do each day. It gives me something to be excited about each morning. To me, there's no way you can keep up your energy day after day, year after year, without exercising. If I go into a football season out of shape, it really affects me.

When I was coaching the Raiders and our team reported to training camp in 1989, I felt as out of shape as I had ever been. With the pressure I felt to succeed, I had been working such long hours that I didn't take the simple and important hour to work out each day. Eventually, it really caught up with me. I didn't look or feel good. I put on ten pounds, my energy level dropped, and so did my performance.

A mere four weeks into our season, when I was suddenly without a job, I found myself with all the time I needed to get back in shape. Since then, even if it is nothing more than a quick fifteen-minute run, exercising has become as much a part of my days as game planning.

On a quiet day two months after our victory over the Atlanta Falcons in Super Bowl XXXIII, a few weeks before we kicked off our annual off-season workout program, each player had a navy hat in his locker that, in white scripted lettering, said, "Always Positive." So simple, yet so important.

It reminds me of our guard Mark Schlereth. Here's a player who since December 1983 has undergone a remarkable twenty-three surgeries, including seventeen on his knees. Yet throughout that time, he has missed only eleven games due to injury. In October 1995, Mark actually passed a kidney stone on a Monday morning and started that night against the Raiders.

Yet even playing hurt, he continues to perform at an unmatched level, being selected to the Pro Bowl during the 1998 season. This guy is so mentally tough, he believes each operation is nothing more than a temporary setback. Doctors tell him it'll take six weeks to rehab his knee, Mark is back in six days.

There even was one time doctors did not expect him back at all. Back in 1993, when Mark was playing for the Washington Redskins, he was stricken with Guillain-Barré syndrome, a possible life-threatening disease that short-circuits the route between the signals sent from the brain to the muscles, causing extreme physical weakness. It tends to move up the body, from your feet, to your thighs, to your hands. It afflicts one out of every 100,000 people.

But Mark was the one and during the setback, there were people telling him he should never play again, he had a great career, it was time to give it up. He refused to listen. He knew that just because some people were offering him an easy way out didn't mean he had to take it.

It's not easy, overcoming Guillain-Barré. Nor is it easy to have knee surgery one day, then spend six hours a day for the next month in the training room going through treatment, improving your leg, getting yourself back in shape. It's a bitch. But Mark always did it with such a positive attitude that he helped not only himself but the rest of the players in our training room.

They were saying, "If Mark can go through all that and still be ready to play each Sunday, what am I complaining about? There's no doubt—I can play."

Like former Broncos head coach John Ralston once said, "Success comes in cans, not in cannots."

STEVE YOUNG

San Francisco 49ers Pro Bowl Quarterback

I define discipline as doing something when there's zero motivation. Discipline is something that Mike Shanahan thrives on. His whole attitude is, "I will outprepare you. I will not be stopped. I will do everything and more to make sure that my men are ready."

It's almost as if he is saying, "We will not lose because of me."

Compared to him, I was lazy when he got ahold of me. Today, you can't mess with my preparation. He taught me to believe that through preparation—not just by a casual glance at your work or even solid preparation, but by deep-penetrating preparation—you are going to be tough to beat. He taught me how to be a better player by not relying only on my athletic ability and natural talents, which most players do, but also on hard work. Add a work ethic to the nth degree to good ability and you're going to be supercharged.

It's the same with him. Mike's got certain innate abilities, but he supercharges them with his attitude to have that unparalleled preparation and work ethic. And what happens is, it becomes a self-fulfilling prophecy. You believe it enough that it actually starts to happen. The impossible catches start to be made. Blocks you can't believe are everywhere. Even the ball will bounce your way when it needs to. It just feeds off itself.

I remember we were in the locker room before Super Bowl XXIX and I said, "Mike, do I know enough? Am I ready to play?" It was so comforting to hear him, the ultimate preparer, say, "Steve you've got it. You're going to smash them." Because people can say that, but when Mike said it, it was like the guru saying "You're there. Just relax." As soon as he said it, I believed it, and look what happened. It was just unbelievable.

He also has an X factor in people skills that you just can't teach. It's innate. It's a combination of motivation and intensity. He understands motivation and how important it is to getting any job done, whether it's winning in football or in business. It's all the same secret, getting people to perform. And he has the ability to do that not only in a small setting with two or three people, but with fifty people. Usually the dynamics of all those people overwhelm somebody, even good people. But not only does Mike not get overwhelmed by it, he thrives on it.

It's an amazing skill, something that he was born with and has mastered over the years. But I've always looked for that in football coaches because it's such a vital skill. And I know there are good football coaches who have pieces of it. But he has a unique ability to get people inspired and motivated.

And then when it comes to winning the game, he has a phenomenal killer instinct. He just knows how to win. He's not scared out there. He has no fear of being successful. A lot of coaches I know, even the successful ones, are wound so tight they try to win 17–14. Mike has no fear of trying to dominate a football game.

He just loves beating on people. He doesn't want to win 14–10. That means nothing to him. He wants to smoke the other guy, and I love that attitude. I remember when he would come into the meetings on Wednesday before we would discuss the game plan. He would say so and so is their defensive coordinator and we are going to smash this guy and this is how we're going to do it. And that's the way he is.

It's funny because it makes me think of the movie *Monty Python and the Holy Grail,* where they cut the guy's legs off because he said, "I'll kick you to death." After they cut his legs off, he says, "I'll bite you to death." That's how Mike is—you can't keep him down. He's one of those guys that if he loses, he's going to seethe inside until he gets back on track.

I loved playing for him. As far as football is concerned, I loved playing for that guy. And his attitude is so contagious to other people, and they don't even know why. But that's the way it is with great motivators. They don't have to stand on the top of a chair and scream at the top of their lungs to motivate you. You're motivated before you even show up at the park. If you need to be motivated the day of the game, you've got some problems. Mike motivates from day one. That's his X factor, and very few people are like that.

After he left our organization [in 1995], I saw John [Elway] and I was still upset about losing Mike. I told him, "You big baby, taking my guy. I hope you got what you wanted." He didn't have to answer. He did.

8

COMPETING
KNOW YOUR ENEMIES

Before the 1998 season, our quarterback John Elway elected to play another season rather than walk away from the game in his blood, as he did in April 1999. As the news of his decision to come back in 1998 spread quickly, the city of Denver and the members of the Broncos organization acted in a celebratory way that confused John.

"Everyone keeps congratulating me for coming back," John said at the June press conference in which he discussed his intention to continue quarterbacking. "The thing is, I never left. The bottom line is, I just wasn't ready to quit competing."

That right there is why John Elway is John Elway. Whether it's in sports or business or anything, the man loves to compete and hates to lose. That's his mindset. And that's why John is as successful as he is. Why do you think he took a chance and invested a couple of million dollars in car dealerships that so many people warned him not to get into? Why did he do it? The man loves a challenge and thrives on competition. Do you think it was accidental that less than ten years after he plunged into dangerous terrain, he sold his car dealerships for $82.5 million? No. The more intense the competition, the tougher the challenge, the better John is.

John is the type of guy who, if you play him in Ping-Pong, air hockey, or racquetball, he has to win—or you stay and you play him the whole night. One time two years ago, I beat him in three straight racquetball games. It felt refreshing, great, satisfying. It felt complete.

"Hey," I told him, starting to walk off the court, "I've had enough."

"No!" he commanded, ready to block the door if necessary. "You're not going anywhere."

So I stayed. And as much I preferred not to, we continued playing. And the only reason we finally quit is that he slammed his racquet into the wall, broke it, and did not have another one to replace it. Otherwise, we might still be playing right now.

John doesn't compete to compete, he competes to win. When he started playing golf after college, a sport he had not attempted before, it wasn't good enough for him to be only adequate. He had to be the best. So he studied the swing as if he was preparing for an exam. He learned its fundamentals as if he was joining the PGA Tour. Mentally, he had a plan for how he would transform himself into a top golfer.

Now, he is a scratch golfer. And he knows the swing so well, he actually could be a golf coach if he wanted.

Through his preparation, through his competitive drive, he can accomplish these types of things in anything in does. You play him at gin rummy—you lose. Everybody thinks gin is a game of luck, but it's a game of memory, knowing cards and knowing your opponent. Studying and focusing the way he does, John always knows his opponent.

And when I go against him—something as challenging as anything I do—I know I'm in for a fight tougher than any other NFL quarterback can provide. Because in all my years of playing sports and coaching them, John Elway is, without question, the greatest competitor I have ever been around.

• • •

As a competent professional, you are capable of being the best in your business. But due to the challenging nature of your industry, it is mandatory that you increase your competence continually—as an individual and as an organization. One of the most effective ways of doing this is employing the same tactics John used in his car business and gin games.

Know your competition. Know them every bit as well as you know yourself.

With the addition of the Cleveland Browns, there are now thirty-one teams in the NFL, and we try to know every one of them inside and out. I don't care if we're playing them in the pre-season or in the Super Bowl, we're going to know everything we can about our competitors. It's almost to the point where we want to be sleeping with the enemy.

I tell our players all the time, "Study your opponents, know their tendencies, concentrate on their strengths and weaknesses. Then, when the game rolls around, you feel like you've studied them so well you can anticipate and visualize what they're going to do before they do it." You start the game ahead of the game.

Sometimes, if you know your competition well enough, you're even able to win games before they're played. An NFL writer conducting an interview in my office asked me midway through the 1996 season, after we already had played Baltimore, why I was studying videotapes of Ravens offensive tackle Tony Jones.

Simple, I explained. For every team, we have a list of players' salaries, enabling us to scan for potential salary-cap victims who might be available down the road. And from studying the list, we knew the Ravens had the league's highest-paid offensive line. We also knew that with all their defensive needs, there was no way they would be able to keep their entire offensive line intact. And with our Pro Bowl offensive tackle Gary Zimmerman planning to retire at the end of the season, we needed a new left tackle to take on all the tough defensive ends we had to compete against in the AFC West.

Six months before we made the trade, Tony Jones became the one offensive tackle we targeted. Sure enough, after the season, we offered a second-round draft choice to Baltimore for Tony and they agreed to the terms of the deal. Since then, Tony has replaced Gary at one of football's most crucial positions and become a Pro Bowl performer himself.

It's out there for you, too, as accessible as the Internet. The knowledge of your competition is available in so many ways, it's a misdemeanor not to use it. There are newspaper and magazine articles on companies and CEOs, their strategies and philosophies advertised for you to see. There are videotapes of their last game or last seminar, just waiting to be plugged into your VCR. There are people leaving various organizations, employees ready to gab away about their former employer's game plans.

Why do you think, year after year, you hear about other teams repeatedly trying to hire away successful assistant coaches from championship teams? Why? They want the winning formula in their organization, the secrets to their competitor's success. It's that simple and that smart.

We have a person living in each NFL city who faxes us every article in the morning newspaper about the team we're facing that week. So each morning when I walk into my office, there already are a stack of newspaper clippings about the opposition that have been slid underneath my door. I sit down at my desk and spend the first forty-five minutes of each morning reading all about my competition. There are reports about injuries to certain players, changes that are being made on the coaching staff, different schemes that are going to be used. The information is devoured and digested quicker than a protein breakfast shake.

Some mornings, I'll admit, the stories almost seem made up. The morning of Super Bowl XXXIII, right around 7:00 A.M., I walked over to my hotel door, picked up my stack of newspaper clippings, glanced down, and was stunned at what I saw: EUGENE ROBINSON ARRESTED FOR SOLICITATION.

I was reading and not believing. Three hours before the Falcons' midnight curfew, Eugene Robinson—the same person who, earlier in the day, won the Bart Starr Award for his "high moral character" from the Christian-based group Athletes in Action—was arrested for reportedly offering forty dollars to an undercover police agent for oral sex. Can you imagine what he was thinking? I know what I was: Eugene Robinson was not going to be as ready for the Super Bowl as our team.

For anyone to say this incident didn't bother the rest of the Falcons is completely ludicrous. It would bother any team. We knew Eugene's mind could not have been 100 percent on the Super Bowl, and we planned to take full advantage of that. We adjusted our game plan and made sure we were going to run as many plays as possible in his direction. We knew the pressure he was under. And if you noticed, during Super Bowl XXXIII, we gained a lot of our yardage after we beat him.

The 80-yard, 2nd-quarter touchdown pass that John threw to Rod Smith beat Eugene. The 39-yard, 4th-quarter swing pass that John threw to Terrell Davis beat Eugene. There were a number of other plays in which we were able to beat Eugene.

The next morning there were more newspaper articles about Eugene. But this time, because we already knew all we needed to about our competition, we were too busy celebrating our victory to read them.

Knowing your competition also means adjusting to it. Because when it comes to competition, there is no such thing as stable anywhere anymore.

No matter what level of success you have achieved, your competition always is trying to overtake you or stay ahead of you. It is a lesson we remember at the end of each season as we gear up for the next one, when we realize people will be shooting at us. We know we have had the AFC's number one offense for the past four seasons, and the question we continually ask ourselves is, "How can we stay at that level?" There's only one way we can.

By being flexible and adjusting to our competition.

You better study the competition because the competition is studying the heck out of you. It's no accident that the offensive formation that we first used three seasons ago—with our normal offensive personnel lining up in a five-wide-receiver set—has shown up all around the league.

By lining up our wide receivers inside and our running backs outside, we were able to see, before the snap, whether the defense would be in man-to-man or zone coverage. The quarterback then was able to get a pre-snap read, giving him a distinct advantage. Now other teams look for that advantage. They have duplicated the formation.

How can we complain? During the off-season, we study all thirty-one teams, really concentrating on the ten best and seeing what they are doing so that we can incorporate it into our offense and defense. Then, shortly after the draft, our focus shifts from our competition to ourselves. We spend the next month trying to see how we can improve. With a microscopic eye, we look at our offense and defense. We break down every play we ran from the season before and see how many yards we averaged on each one.

We might have 50 different running plays, 200 different passing plays, and they fall into different categories: red zone, short yardage, goal line, third downs, and so forth. Then we say, "Okay, this is where we've been effective and this is where we haven't."

In the ineffective areas, we want to know, Why are we ineffective? Is it the play? The players? Is it the execution? From there, we come up with a plan so that once we go to training camp the following summer, we're able to adjust and make things as difficult as possible for our opponents.

It baffles me that so many people fail to counter what their competitors are doing. It's right in front of them, and they're somehow blind to it. Just last February, Levi's—which emerged as the dominant outfitter of the baby-boom generation in the 1960s—had to slash its work force. The San Francisco-based Levi's, whose brands include Dockers and Slate, announced it was going to shut down 11 of its 22 plants in the United States and Canada and lay off 5,900 workers—30 percent of its North American workforce.

Why? Department store chains such as Sears and J.C. Penney produced their own private-label brands of denim clothing. Other retailers ranging from J. Crew to Brooks Brothers came out with their own jean lines. Fashion companies like Tommy Hilfiger and FUBU began carving out niches among teens in the denim market. Unionbay introduced its own jean line. And the Gap and Old Navy convinced kids it was cool to wear khaki.

Over time, fashion shifted and diversified, and Levi's didn't. It cost them. Levi's went from top to bottom, proving the point that no one stays where they're at. In the constant life battle to progress or regress, you always must strive to be better. If not, the consequences are readily understandable.

Somebody is passing you by.

As a little kid, I had always heard about what a great chess player my grandfather was, how tough he was to beat. People held his chess skills in such high regard, they feared taking him on. But one day, right about the time I was in fifth grade, I decided to go up against him.

It was, as you might expect, no contest. But not in the way you might think. On my fourth maneuver of the game, I beat him. I got him with a move called fool's mate, a maneuver I had studied. It was a very basic, very strategic move, but he had never seen it before. He was concentrating on another move, I really kind of got him off-balance, and he was a little embarrassed. And I was thrilled.

Right then I realized that so many of the competitors you face are not as invincible as people make them out to be. Was Levi's invincible? Was Duke in the 1999 college basketball tournament? No. And neither is your competitor.

What you must remember to factor in is that the better the competition is, the better you are going to perform. This is what competition does. It forces you to elevate your performance to levels you might have thought unattainable. So don't ever be in awe of anyone.

People are people, and when I got my first NFL coaching job as the Broncos' receivers coach in 1984, I didn't realize that. I came into the league and saw these incredible coaching legends—Chicago's Mike Ditka, San Francisco's Bill Walsh, Pittsburgh's Chuck Noll, Dallas's Tom Landry, Miami's Don Shula—and told myself, "Darn, those coaches are incredibly tough to beat. How are we ever going to do it?"

Maybe I thought that way because I didn't believe I was worthy of attaining their success. Now, after learning what I have, I say, "Why not?" You have to feel good about your preparation, your organization; you've got to believe that you are better than anybody else out there. Not in an outward, cocky sense, but in a quiet, confident manner. You have to believe that the only way you will lose is if you are not prepared to win.

In my first statement at my first team meeting with the Broncos in 1995, I told them we could beat anybody. We could win the Super Bowl. I said, If we are going to be the underdog, why not make the most of it? Let's be the Pekingese that's barking at the German shepherd. But once you start giving somebody too much respect, then you become inferior because you're assuming they are better than you.

I see it in other teams' attitudes toward us now. During the 1998 season, it happened against Philadelphia, it happened against Dallas. They saw us score a couple of touchdowns early in the game and they instantly began telling themselves, "Here we go again." Instead of fighting back, they have a built-in excuse to lose.

Meanwhile, we're telling our team to put away the competitor, to embarrass them. The mindset is not just to win, but to win with everybody playing the perfect game. We don't want to simply hold our position. That's not good enough for a successful organization. We'll let the opponent hold its position.

Winners, even against insurmountable odds, are attacking day and night.

In Super Bowl XXXIII, not only was I sure about how we would react, I was sure about how the Falcons would react. We knew them. We felt there was nothing they could do to surprise us. Well before the game, during our week of preparations, I even predicted to my son not only who was going to win the game, but who was going to win the game's Most Valuable Player award.

I knew going into the game that with the way the Falcons

played defense, John Elway or Shannon Sharpe would be the Super Bowl XXXIII MVP. I told Kyle it was highly unlikely that Terrell Davis was going to be MVP because I knew going in what type of front seven and what type of safety support the Falcons had on their run defense.

We couldn't have T.D. run the ball 25 to 30 times; he wasn't going to gain 150 to 200 yards. That plan had less to do with T.D.'s talent than with the fact that the Falcons were just too fast and too consistent with their run defense. We could have challenged them, but if we did that, we risked raising their confidence. They were geared to stop the run. So we decided that the best way to beat the Falcons was through the air.

We managed to get some big passing plays. We softened up their defense a little bit, then came back in the second half with a whole new game plan that included more of the running game. It was not accidental that in the first half, John threw for 199 yards and his only touchdown, which turned out to be the final touchdown of his illustrious career.

Where my predictions were wildly off were in regard to Shannon. On our first series of the game, in which he caught two passes for 26 yards, Shannon sprained his left knee and could not play the rest of the game. And unbeknown to me, after the game, Kyle pulled aside Shannon with a little memorable message.

"Too bad you got hurt," Kyle told Shannon. "My dad told me he thought you might have been the MVP of the game."

But my other prediction, which came from knowing and adjusting to our competition, was right on. John Elway, the greatest competitor I have known, was selected Super Bowl XXXIII's Most Valuable Player.

Having a clear understanding of your competitor's strengths and weaknesses, their strategies and tactics, will provide you with a renewed feeling of confidence, not unlike the one we feel with each victory.

But it's tough work, knowing your competition. Then again, it's tough work being a champion.

GEORGE SEIFERT

Former San Francisco 49ers
and Current Carolina Panthers Head Coach

Everybody has to be a competitor to be in this business. Bill Walsh is a great competitor; so are Ray Rhodes and Mike Holmgren. But there's something unique about Mike. His competitiveness is so subtle that it might be stronger than anybody else's I know.

I still remember one year we were together at San Francisco and had to coach the NFC team in the 1993 Pro Bowl. Well, when we lost the game, the emotion that he demonstrated was unique. For most coaches, it's not a tragedy; it's an all-star game. You don't like to lose in anything, but Mike treated it like it was almost catastrophic. From that point on, I knew something was different about his intensity and his competitive drive.

I can't say I really understood his uniqueness until maybe after he left San Francisco, to be honest with you. Now that I look back on it, I knew that he was special and very good, but as far as how good he was, sometimes you need the distance to look back at the different people you worked with. And he stands out as a special guy.

It was a tough situation for him when he first became a head coach with the Raiders and he didn't succeed. But he didn't feel sorry for himself. He just went back to work to become the best at running the San Francisco offense at that time. When he came on, we said, "Here's what we want you to do. We want you to study this offense and get the total insight into it and then we want you to implement it."

He stuck through it to the core until he developed a real understanding of what we did. In a short period of time, he was an expert.

Once he understood the system, he started tweaking it a little bit to improve it. His play-calling was different, throwing opponents off-balance. That helped us win.

But there are other things that make him a successful coach. With his knowledge, he had an insight into the movement and the art form of attacking defenses. No one did it like him.

He probably has the best insight into the passing game and natural sense for the running game of anyone I know. We threw the ball often and he had a more than normal knowledge of the passing game. A lot of offensive coaches might really be into the running game; he knew the running game as well. He made it a point to know everything he could.

9

COMMUNICATING
THE POWER OF BEING CONNECTED

This was the last thing I was expecting. But at the NFL owners meetings in Phoenix in March 1999, who should walk right up to me, smiling, talking, acting like he's my best friend? None other than Dan Reeves, my former boss in Denver and the current Atlanta Falcons head coach.

Dan comes right over to me as if he didn't criticize me two months earlier, didn't fire me eight years ago, didn't charge me with insubordination, didn't try to tarnish my coaching reputation. He shakes my hand and acts like there never has been a single problem between us.

And I'm going, This guy's got to be frickin' crazy.

But then, that's Dan. The man knows a lot about winning, but not as much about communicating.

Exhibit A: After the 1991 season, when the Denver Broncos came within three points of upsetting the Buffalo Bills in the AFC championship game, Dan called me into his office for a meeting I won't ever forget.

"Mike," he told me as he sat behind his desk, "I want to run the offense. It's very important for me to be the guy calling the plays. I know that's what you want to do, and that's what you should do. So I have to make some changes because I want to do it. I'm afraid with your personality and my personality, it's not going to work out. Sorry."

We shook hands, and that was it. I was out on the street again. Fired.

Now, understand. I don't have a problem with Dan firing me. That was his right. He was the head coach, and he did what he felt was in the best interests of his team. How can you argue with that? But what I did have a problem with, as a matter of professional courtesy, was the fact that he waited a whole week after the season to let me go.

Had he fired me the day after our season ended—and I'm guessing he knew he was going to get rid of me all along—then I might have had the chance to interview for any one of the five offensive coordinator jobs that were then open. But by the time he got around to cutting me loose, the only two offensive coordinator jobs open were Pittsburgh's and San Francisco's.

But even worse? A week after he fired me, somebody leaked a story to the *Denver Post* that forever changed our relationship. The source and the story accused me of being insubordinate. It said one of the main reasons I was fired was because behind Dan's back, I was scripting plays with our quarterback John Elway.

This violated my strongly held beliefs on the consistency of communication: If you have something on your mind, get it off your chest. But Dan didn't. That's when I lost all respect for him.

Aside from not being honest, these accusations lacked substance. Let me tell you why. When you're an offensive coordinator and you know what plays your quarterback likes and doesn't like, you try to give him those plays. I knew John's top twenty, twenty-five plays. There wasn't any order to them, there wasn't any scripting involved. None. John would just call the plays he wanted. Somehow, this got turned into some kind of wacky conspiracy theory.

To this day, everyone still has his own interpretation of what happened. But the bottom line, as indisputable as John's Hall of Fame credentials, is this: Not once during my time with Dan did I suspect he was unhappy with or distrustful of me. He simply didn't communicate this to me, so I was completely in the dark. Had he been more open with me, maybe I could have addressed his concerns.

Were it not for all the circumstances and people involved, I still might think the problem was me. But Dan didn't communicate with his quarterback, either.

When I returned to Denver, one philosophy that I attempted to make abundantly clear to every member of our organization was that they might not always like what I had to say, but at least they knew I was always going to tell the truth.

Face it: Without truth, there can be no trust. Without trust, there can be no relationship. And without a relationship, the chances of achieving success decrease dramatically.

Isn't it interesting how the trio of truth, trust, and relationships are tied so closely to communication? Even today, amid all the lawyers, accountants, and bankers of this great global economy, multimillion-dollar deals still are made with nothing more than a verbal commitment. One side offers one thing, another side offers another, and through an exchange of decent proposals and honest words comes a handshake and an agreement.

It is why the importance of being true to your word, of saying what you mean and meaning what you say, cannot be stressed enough.

With ethical performances and honest answers, through fulfilling promises and demonstrating loyalty, layers of trust are built. They are built thick enough to be virtually impenetrable. People listen to those whom they trust. They give them loyalty and respect. Their word is their bond.

Once you break that bond, you're asking for trouble. And chances are, you're going to get it. Your name will be damaged. Your reputation will be scarred. And a poor reputation can be tougher to overcome than a costly turnover. Sometimes even the most persistent and hard-working individuals are unable to do it.

Before it ever gets to that, take the proper and necessary steps to avoid it. Repeatedly ask yourself if you are doing the right thing. If not, stop yourself, revise your behavior, alter your plan. But make sure that your actions are as sincere as your word. Otherwise you will find yourself in a situation you regret, maybe not entirely unlike the one that we'll refer to as Exhibit B: Dan and John Elway.

On an unseasonably chilly fall morning in 1991 in Denver, Dan angrily summoned me into his second-floor office at Broncos headquarters. Once I got there, he threw the *Denver Post* sports section at me.

"How'd this story get in there?" he yelled.

Dan was referring to a front page detailed story about the strained relationship between the head coach and the quarterback. Everyone in town—coaches, reporters, friends, family—knew about it, but no one had gone public. Until then. That morning, the late great *Denver Post* sports columnist Dick Connor had penned a column telling of John's unhappiness with Dan, how the two didn't get along, how they didn't even talk anymore.

I looked at the story and shrugged. "I didn't give the media this story, Dan. And why are you yelling at me? I had nothing to do with it. I've been trying to keep this relationship intact. Why not talk to John? He's the one who said this, not me."

So many times people think yelling at somebody heightens their level of respect. In fact, it is just the opposite. In my experience, I have found that a gentle word or warm smile—two things I'm still trying do more often—can do far more good than any verbal diatribe.

But Dan was furious with me, thinking I should have found a way to prevent the story from getting out. To help defuse the situation, I went downstairs to the weight room, interrupted John's training session, and brought him back upstairs with me. My solution was to get them to finally communicate.

To me, if you've got a problem, you've got to hit it head-on. Otherwise little things turn into big things. Dan didn't hit it head-on, though. He waited, waited, and let his and John's anger fester. This meeting was the only time he openly communicated with John. They were more than ready to hash out some of the differences that had become an incessant distraction to our team and our personal lives.

"Now, John," I started, "why don't you tell Dan why you don't like him. And Dan, why don't you tell John why you don't like him."

For the next thirty minutes, John and Dan attacked each other. It wasn't really loud—it was matter-of-fact. In hard, angry voices, each stated his argument. John didn't think Dan's offensive system was capable of winning a Super Bowl. Dan didn't think John could pick up his offense well enough to win a Super Bowl. John didn't like the rumors Dan was spreading about him and the way he was always patronizing him. Dan didn't like John's attitude toward him personally and professionally.

On and on it went, everything getting out in the open. It was good because it had been burning inside both of them for years and years.

Now there is no way to prove this, but I believe this as much as I believe in preparation: After that thirty-minute venting session, Dan had no more use for me. Up until then, I had been his conduit to John. I was the only way he could get through to him, because they never communicated. The only time they did was the one November morning when I brought them together to speak with each other. But now that they had channeled their frustrations, now that they had shared their problems and differences, Dan didn't need me around any longer.

That was okay. To me it was worth it, because the only chance I felt we had to get back to the Super Bowl that season was to address the problems right then and there.

After Dan got rid of me, and after I accepted the offensive coordinator's job in San Francisco with the 49ers, I brought along the ideas that I had formed from watching the way Dan handled his relationship with John. It didn't take long to realize that consistent communication is closely correlated to consistent winning.

We had a standout running back, Ricky Watters, who now plays for the Seattle Seahawks. If you didn't tell Ricky how many times he was going to carry the football on Sunday, his temperament would get the best of him. He would explode during the game. It got so bad that 49ers quarterback Steve Young would kick Ricky out of the huddle because he could become a detriment to the rest of the team.

What we decided to do was hit the problem head-on. Each Friday before the game, I would sit down with Ricky and explain to him, in detail, our offensive game plan. If we were planning to throw the ball more on Sunday, I would tell Ricky he was going to be carrying the ball less, maybe twelve to fifteen times. If we were going to run the ball on Sunday, I would tell Ricky he was going to be carrying the ball more, maybe twenty or twenty-three times. As long as our intentions were well communicated and everything was out in the open, then Ricky understood. He went from becoming an "I" guy to a "we" guy, somebody whom Steve Young and the rest of the 49ers offense depended on heavily.

In Super Bowl XXIX in Miami, Ricky was more effective as a receiver than a runner, just as we told him he would be. He scored three touchdowns—one on the ground, two through the air. We couldn't have won without him.

Interestingly enough, after our super season in San Francisco, Ricky and I both left the 49ers. I went to Denver, he went to Philadelphia. And early in the season, stories started filtering out of Philadelphia that Ricky was all upset with how much he was carrying the ball, how he should be made a bigger part of the offense.

Reading the newspaper clippings, I laughed to myself. I actually considered calling Eagles head coach Ray Rhodes—who also worked with us in San Francisco in 1994 as the 49ers defensive coordinator—to tell him how to solve the problem. All he had to do was sit down with Ricky the Friday before the game and explain to him how much or how little he would be getting the call.

I was about to pick up the telephone to call Ray when the thought hit me: The Broncos were scheduled to play the Eagles on November 12 of that season. Quick as I could, I hung up the phone, not wanting to jeopardize our chances of beating Philadelphia.

A lot of good that did. Ricky caught four passes, rushed for two touchdowns, and the Eagles still beat us, 31–13.

Communicating might be the single most important skill we possess, and it has many forms: reading, writing, listening, speaking. Think about how often you do each of the four things in a given day, how important they are to your daily and lifelong performance.

But communicating isn't all about talking. Just as much, it's about listening.

There's a reason each of us was given two ears and one tongue. We're supposed to listen more than we talk. Yet you'd be surprised. Some people just love to hear themselves. They try to overpower people with their personalities and words. But sometimes the most powerful people are the ones who simply sit back and listen.

It makes a lot of sense, when you think about it. You don't learn from talking; you learn from listening. Last time I checked, I never said anything I didn't already know.

Listening does not just constitute doing it for a few moments. Listen to entire thoughts. Wait until people finish their sentences. Do not interrupt them. When they are done, then take your turn. Becoming a better listener allows you to be more patient and the others around you to be happier and more productive. They feel as though you respect their thoughts and wishes. In return, you get loyalty and a heightened sense of respect.

Our coaching staff always meets with our players and listens to what they have to say about our work environment. Shortly after the 1995 season, in which we finished 8–8, I met with each player to solicit input on how each one thought we could improve the atmosphere at work.

Pro Bowl guard Mark Schlereth, who had won a Super Bowl with the Washington Redskins during the 1991 season, spoke glowingly of how his former coach Joe Gibbs fostered camaraderie in the most simple yet effective manner: If his players won on Sunday, he would give them off Monday.

Ordinarily, this is not done around the league. Mondays are used for running, lifting, meeting. But the more I thought about what Mark said, the more sense it made. We adopted the practice in 1996. That season we finished 13–3.

Now it would be ludicrous to suggest that our success is directly tied to a bonus day off that most players on most teams don't get. But it helps. Every little bit does when you are trying to gain that competitive advantage.

There is only one way to improve and stay on top: when you can accept ideas from other people and listen to what they say. When you listen to another person's concerns and suggestions, it alerts you to possibilities that you might not have considered. Even bizarre ideas might have something useful in them if you just give them a chance.

During our talk after the 1995 season, Mark also suggested that the players, coaches, and their wives and girlfriends somehow find a way to become friendlier. The way they did it in Washington was with a party at a player's house. I said, "Hey, that's a great idea." But I didn't want the party to be at a player's house. I wanted it to be at mine.

So each year for the past three years, the week before we play our first regular season game, I have invited over all the coaches, players, wives, and girlfriends for a night of mirth and merriment. We set up a Las Vegas-style casino, with blackjack and roulette, and little prizes for the biggest winners. We have karaoke machines, catered food, unlimited drinks. The parties have been scheduled from seven to ten, and usually go until one-thirty in the morning. We practically have to kick everyone out.

But the point is made. The coaches, players, wives, and girlfriends think, "Here's a guy who will really look out after us." I will, and it makes guys want to go out and do anything they can to help the organization win.

Now, I try to listen to the things my players like. I remember some of the meetings we used to have when I was an assistant coach for the Broncos, and Dan would ask what plays John would feel comfortable and uncomfortable running. As soon as I would tell Dan what plays John didn't like, he instantly would get mad at me.

"Why doesn't he like it?" Dan would demand to know.

I didn't know—all I knew was that he didn't. And what difference did it make why he didn't like them? The bottom line was that he was not confident running those plays, and we wanted our quarterback to be as confident as possible.

I used to ask our offensive coordinator Gary Kubiak that all the time: what plays did John not like? If there were five plays that John didn't like and they were my five favorite plays, it didn't matter. If he didn't like them and I couldn't explain them well enough to where he felt comfortable enough to run those plays, I had to go in a different direction. Otherwise it's suicide.

That's how we beat the Falcons in the Super Bowl. Three of the plays John didn't like were my favorite ones, plays I thought would work. But if I had called any of those plays, John would not have been confident wondering, "Why is he running a play he knows I'm not comfortable with?" Why even go there? It's not worth it. So the plays were scrapped, John was confident, and it showed in his performance.

While listening, it's a good idea not to be thin-skinned. It is a must with so many jobs. I'll listen to the criticism that comes at me in the newspapers or on TV. But if you lose your concentration because somebody says something negative about you, then you have fallen into the biggest trap there is: ego.

It's not easy when someone is being critical of you to sit back and listen. It happened with me when I was an assistant with the Broncos and Dan went after my name and reputation. Did it hurt? Yeah. Did I have to grin and bear it for a long time? Yeah. Did I think it was wrong? Yeah.

But I said, Someday I'll get a chance to explain what really happened. Now that I have paid some dues as an assistant coach and now that I have become a head coach, I can defend myself. I can communicate my feelings. And it amazes me that even today, after all this has happened, Dan still has never said one word to me about it. He can walk up to me at an NFL owners meeting, pretend nothing happened, and carry on as if everything were normal. Me, I don't know how people operate that way.

Though I was unable to connect with Dan, I used the lessons he inadvertently taught me to connect with others. These lessons provide the unlimited ability to improve the environment in which you work and live.

JOE MONTANA

Former San Francisco 49ers and Kansas City Chiefs Quarterback

On the practice field there were a couple of things that I noticed about Mike right away. One was his willingness to attack a defense. He did not want to sit back and relax when the game was on the line, which is what most coaches look to do.

They'd say, "Well, we'll just sit it out here until the clock runs down." Mike wasn't like that. He loved to attack.

He had a great flair for making little changes to our offense to make it better. Some of the routes and patterns were changed slightly just to affect the defense a little bit more, and even the slightest bit of movement made a difference.

I played under Mike for only one season, and I wasn't really permitted around there (with my elbow injury) much until I could practice. That's not very well known, and Mike might not even know that, but they didn't want me around. They thought I would be a distraction. So I just did what I was told. And early on I didn't get to spend as much time around Mike as I would have liked. But still, it didn't take very long to realize what made him effective.

The biggest thing was his willingness to listen to what the guys playing the position talked about. There were all these little things that looked good on paper that sometimes needed a little touch, and Mike was always one of those guys you could talk to about them. He wasn't someone who preached at you, he talked to you, then tried to work things out the best way possible.

This is an important trait from a quarterback's point of view because you're on an island, like a cornerback, and no one really knows what takes place out there. No one else understands the game from the quarterback's perspective. It's always funny hearing some of the former offensive linemen on television talking about the game. I say, "Well, what does he know about the game because he sees it from a wide-angle lens or with his head stuck up somebody's rear end most of the day?"

One of the things Mike always talked about was his relationship with John Elway, and I think it really blossomed when he came back to Denver. A lot of it has to do with their ability to know what's going on and communicate about things that happen and make those changes, then have faith in each other. And it's not just with John. I think you see that when Bubby Brister comes in. Bubby struggled for a while and then he comes in and he's able to take over, and that all carries over from Mike.

Anyone who can communicate like Mike does has to be more effective at what he does.

10

LEADING OUT IN FRONT

No matter what business you're in, the principles of leadership are the same.

A real leader must produce, thus putting himself in a position where others look to him for guidance, for advice, for an example of how to behave. Any person who follows the strategies in this book puts himself in a position to be a successful leader.

A real leader must be bold enough to stand alone. This is not an easy thing to do. Late in the third quarter of Super Bowl XXXII, with the score tied at 17 and Denver facing a 3rd-and-6 at the Green Bay Packers' 12-yard line, our quarterback John Elway dropped back to pass, found no one open, and began running down the middle of the field. He veered right, only to find Packers safeties LeRoy Butler and Mike Prior waiting for him.

Now, most quarterbacks know how vital it is to protect themselves and to stay healthy. But most quarterbacks aren't John Elway. Rather than sliding short of the first down or running out of bounds, John fearlessly dove with the weight of three lopsided Super Bowl losses, and the desire for one Super Bowl win, propelling him.

He was hit so hard, he spun around like a helicopter. But when he landed, he had gained a decisive first down and the momentum needed for the Broncos to win their first-ever Super Bowl. In a career full of them, it was, if you ask me, John's single most memorable play. It had to be. He had no blockers in front of him, yet he still was willing to stand alone, to jump alone, to lead his team to a previously unreached destination.

You can talk about teamwork, you can talk about sharing the load, you can talk about spreading it around all you want. But at some point, your leader has to emerge. Ours did. And when he did, the rest of our team followed right along. That, ultimately, is what leaders do. They guide you along the way, to your short- and long-term destinations.

A real leader must be empowered with the courage to make difficult decisions. It also is not an easy thing to do. How many times have you had to tell someone you were dismissing them from their job? Or shifting their responsibilities to a different area? People do not want to hear these kinds of things, but as a leader, you have to be strong enough to tell them.

The toughest decision I've ever had to make as a head coach happened a mere two weeks after we beat the Atlanta Falcons in the Super Bowl. We were getting ready to leave for the annual college scouting combine in Indianapolis, where we test and interview prospective draftees, when our eight-time Pro Bowl safety and defensive captain Steve Atwater dropped by our training complex. He visited our defensive coordinator, Greg Robinson, and defensive backs coach, Ed Donatell, inquiring about his future.

Steve was smart enough to know that we were scheduled to pay him $3 million in 1999 and that we were pressed up against the NFL-imposed salary cap. It was going to be tough to fit him into our salary structure. He asked Greg and Ed, "Am I going to be here? What's my status for next year?"

In all honesty, our initial plan was to wait until March 1st, when we would have asked Steve to take a salary reduction to give us more flexibility under the salary cap. If he opposed the idea, then he could have looked for another team or retired.

But the more I thought about it, and the more I agonized over it, the more I realized that decisive action had to be taken. It could not wait, not when Steve had brought the issue to a head. The question was, "Where do we go from here?" For every leader in any field, that is always the question, the problem, and the challenge, all mixed together. As a leader, you can't just live in the present. You constantly have to think about the future as well.

It would have been so simple to temporarily sweep the problem underneath the rug. It certainly would have made things easier on me and the organization for a little while. But that would not have been fair to Steve. So, in what was the most difficult decision I've had to make in my first four years as Broncos coach, I decided to cut Steve.

There was so much emotion involved; I cared so much for the guy. But the decision was best for all parties. We saved money we needed, Steve had a chance to shop himself as an unrestricted free agent, and he wound up signing a three-year, $8.2 million contract with the New York Jets.

Is it easy picturing Steve in kelly green and white, especially with the Jets scheduled to play in Denver at Mile High Stadium during the 1999 season? No. Was it the right thing for him and our team? Absolutely.

As a leader, you are responsible for everything that occurs within your organization. If you notice a problem, you have to become a problem-solver. You have to act swiftly and decisively. Otherwise, you jeopardize the success of your organization. But when it comes to being a real leader, even more is required. A real leader must demonstrate the compassion to listen to and help others. One of the things I've watched over the years is how power changes people. It never ceases to amaze me. Once a person is promoted to boss, once he wields a heavy hammer, he often forgets where he came from. He forgets the same problems he had when he was an assistant, trying to climb the organizational ladder. This is one of a leader's biggest booby traps.

To me, the people working for you, the people who share in the stressful environment we all inhabit, must know you care about them. If people know you care about them, they will be more willing to go into battle for you. If there's no understanding or compassion for an employee's valid personal issues, a polluted atmosphere is created in which the employee and employer are both disgruntled. It snowballs as each side becomes more and more upset with the other. One need look no further than John Elway and Dan Reeves.

Avoid this. Head it off before it becomes a problem. Talk to your employees. You'd be surprised at how much it might help.

Within our organization, our wide receivers coach, Mike Heimerdinger, once needed some financial assistance, even though he never would ask for it. When Mike left his job as offensive coordinator at Duke University to come to Denver in 1995, he got stuck holding mortgages on two houses, one in North Carolina, the other in Colorado. With two house payments, Mike's wife, Kathie, had to take a part-time job to help defray the costs.

When I found out his wife was working when she should have been at home with their daughter, Alicia, and their son, Brian, I put a stop to that as quickly as I could. I loaned Mike $30,000 for the year—until he could sell his house in North Carolina. He sold the house, he paid back the money, and we went on. As much as Mike might have appreciated the money, I believe he appreciated the compassion considerably more.

This game is so competitive—any business is so competitive—and often it's a stressful environment. I just think people need to know that you care about them. You will breed trust, which in turn breeds loyalty, a trait cherished in any organization.

Because of loyalty, we have not had a single coordinator or position coach leave our coaching staff during my first four seasons as a head coach in Denver. One reason we've had so much stability is the job conditions. They know exactly where I'm coming from all the time. I tell them how much time they can have off during the spring and summer, I tell them what I expect them to get done in the office, I tell them the only games we're going to play are the ones on Sunday.

But maybe most important, they know that if they fight for me, I'm going to fight for them. When I was an assistant coach, I never worked with the insecurity of a one-year contract, and as long as I'm coaching the Broncos, none of my assistants ever will, either. In fact, sixteen of our assistant coaches received three-year contract extensions in March. They know as long as they take care of me, I'll take care of them.

I guess it's no surprise, then, that during each of the past two off-seasons, when Mike Heimerdinger has had offers to become offensive coordinator for the San Diego Chargers and Dallas Cowboys in 1998 and the Jacksonville Jaguars in 1999, he rejected each one.

A real leader knows everything going on within his or her organization. That is why you must attend business meetings, company functions, any situation where your presence can ensure that the proper atmosphere will prevail. It is a leader's responsibility to always be in touch with the mood of his collective organization, as well as the mood of his individual employees.

Sometimes it is not what it should be. And then it is up to the leader to step in and bring it back to its intended level.

An example: Our first-round draft choice in 1997, defensive tackle Trevor Pryce. During his rookie season, Trevor was always late, an action I consider to be completely disrespectful. We must have fined him $15,000 his rookie year for lateness.

Then there was the time in October 1997 when our team was scheduled to fly to Buffalo on a Saturday morning for a game against the Bills. A mammoth snowstorm blasted Denver. We got hit with about twenty-two inches of snow. Players trickled into our training facility all day long, fighting the conditions, covered with snow. Some even arrived on their snowmobiles. Every player managed to get there.

Every player, that is, except one. Trevor decided to stay home. Just not come. We couldn't get him on the phone and finally we just left Denver without him.

Now, it's a leader's job to try all possible ways to motivate an employee. Some guys learn through gentle teaching, some through constant repetition, some through severe penalties. We tried everything with Trevor. We fined him. We met with him. We yelled at him. Nothing worked. So after his rookie season ended, I called him into my office for about the tenth time and told him that if he didn't want to abide by our rules, he'd be out of a job.

Then every day during the off-season, we had a coach call him. Every day. "What time are you going to be here, Trevor? Why weren't you here today, Trevor?" We were all over him.

Finally, a light just went on in his head. He realized it was easier to do the work and be accountable than put up with the constant pressure and the barrage of phone calls from our organization. From that point, he started to grow up. He realized that this wasn't Clemson anymore, this was real life. He became a professional and, not coincidentally, one of the top defensive tackles in the NFL.

Eventually, you might be so tough with your employees, you begin irritating them. Unfortunately, this happens. But as long as you have demonstrated the ability to lead them, they are going to demonstrate the ability to follow you.

Look at what happened in Miami right after the 1998 season ended. Dolphins coach Jimmy Johnson wanted to retire. But who was the first guy at his office door in the morning? Dan Marino. The same Dan Marino who has been known not to get along with Jimmy.

Dan was there because he knows Jimmy can help him win. Jimmy has won Super Bowls already. Dan hasn't. Through his actions, Dan said, If you give me your best, I'll give you my best, and together we'll help get the Dolphins to the championship. Jimmy decided he would stay. How could he not?

Growing up, my impressions were that leaders were supposed to be the big guys with the loud mouths. But through the years, I have learned there is a lot more to it. George Seifert, who used to be the San Francisco 49ers head coach and now holds the same title for the Carolina Panthers, was the most peaceful leader I've ever encountered.

George was not a guy who was going to pat his players on the back and tell them what a great job they were doing. His mindset was that he expected them to do a great job. He knew that production counted for a lot more than conversation. But with the way he led, people were willing to follow him.

When I think back to some of the finest leaders I have known—George, Cleveland Browns president Carmen Policy—I've noticed that they have found a way to be both warm enough and distant enough to the soldiers in their armies. It is the perfect area in which to position yourself.

You don't want to be too close to your employees because you need room to be objective enough to make clear-headed decisions. Then again, you don't want your employees or anyone in your organization to think you were right behind Scrooge when they handed out warmth.

If you are a real leader, there is one other point to remember: You will lead a short and bumpy life. One week you can be acclaimed the Einstein of your field, the next week you can be hailed as one of the dumbest people on the face of the earth, and the following week, you can be back to genius again. It is nothing more than the fickle nature of our society.

As a leader, you must always show that you cannot be intimidated—by anyone or anything. Yet there will be times when you will be challenged. During the 1994 season, when the San Francisco 49ers were opening the season at home on a Monday night against the Oakland Raiders, we faced one of those situations during pregame warm-ups.

Out on the field, about 25 yards from where our offense was warming up, our players were complaining that Raiders owner Al Davis was standing on our side of the field, limiting the area where our receivers could run their patterns. Our players were complaining about it, and with good reason. So I pulled aside one of our quarterbacks, Elvis Grbac, and gave him some unusual instructions.

"If you happen to throw the ball in that direction," I said, pointing to where Al was standing, "I wouldn't get mad at you."

Elvis grinned and then, on the ensuing play, threw a hard, tight spiral toward Al. At the last moment, Al noticed the incoming missile and desperately lunged out of its way. His hair, normally greased back, was all out of place, standing straight up like a rooster's. Then when Al looked back to see where the football had come from, and saw our team looking in his direction and laughing, he slid up his middle finger and thrust it in our direction.

The action I called for might seem petty; yet it served a purpose. Since then, I can honestly say that I never have noticed Al standing on the field during pregame warmups again. And it showed him and our team that we wouldn't back down to anyone or anything.

But that also raises another instructional point about leadership. Your employees look to you for control. If you demonstrate that you can handle anything, they too will have the same feeling.

It's why I knew how much trouble Chargers quarterback Ryan Leaf was going to have during his rookie season in 1998, when he exploded at a reporter for something insignificant that showed up in the newspaper. What does that indicate? He loses control at tense moments. If that's the case, what's going to happen when he's down in the fourth quarter? Is he going to lose it then, too? As the leader of the offense, the Chargers had better hope not.

It's not easy when people take their shots, but it's how you react that matters. Are you in control or out of control? A leader—whether it's a quarterback, a CEO, or a department head—must always be in control. And he must always be productive. That, to me, is as important as any of a leader's traits. People look to people who are productive. Once the production level drops off, so does their leadership.

So many times it will feel as if the rent is coming due, the castle is being stormed, the situation is deteriorating right before your eyes. But just remember to stand tall, to be courageous, to be compassionate, to tell it like it is. In the end, the things that matter most are the opinions of you and your employees, and your records of accomplishment.

They lead the way.

CARMEN POLICY

Cleveland Browns President

I'll never forget when I first saw Mike in action. My reaction was, "This guy would have made a great trial lawyer—analyzing the issues, seeing what's ahead of him, recognizing the obstacles, preparing to the nth detail, and realizing what has to be accomplished and how he should go about doing that in dealing with every piece of evidence and every witness."

And then it hit me. I realized, that's the secret for success in any business, in any situation where leadership is required, and that could be the military or politics. The secret is the attributes that Mike embodies.

That's why I think Shanahan could be not only a great football name, it could be a great political or military name, because of what he brings to the table. He brings to every challenge not only his foresight, but also his willingness to commit everything in his being—everything—to the task of getting the job done.

He possesses a rare combination of toughness, expertise, naked intelligence, street sense, and terrific people skills. Now think of it for a moment. When do you see all those attributes rolled up into one individual? Normally you'll find them in a great leader of a nation or a tremendous CEO of a global company. But Mike Shanahan has somehow put them all together and just happens to be coaching a football team.

Mike has a quiet confidence about him. He doesn't get flustered or in any way frazzled, no matter what's being said to him or about him. Yet the self-confidence he has doesn't make him too arrogant. It causes people who are working with him to really feel as though the situation is under control.

I noticed that early on when he was with us at the 49ers (when I was the president there) and in the process of developing a reputation for what he was doing to our offense, he never let it appear, though, that he was taking any of the credit personally. It was always "us, the players, Steve Young, Jerry Rice, Ricky Watters, the assistant coaches, that Gary Kubiak is doing a wonderful job."

He also is a great listener. You ask his opinion, he'll lay it out for you and he won't hesitate to give you what he's thinking and why he's thinking it. But if he's in an environment where he gets the slightest sense that there's something to be learned, he'll be as quiet as a church mouse. Then, down the road, that knowledge will emerge.

I'll never forget when we first got started with the 49ers. He wasn't satisfied just being offensive coordinator in the sense that that would be the only challenge he would take on. In his first year with us in 1992, he started looking at personnel and seeing how we ran the operation and how we negotiated contracts and how we dealt with logistics. In 1993, they started talking about the salary cap and free agency and he would sit with me and we would discuss things relative to them at length.

When we would do a contract, he would come in and say, "Now why exactly did you do this contract this way?" And you never had to explain it more than once. And usually you didn't even have to finish explaining. You could sense he was catching on halfway through. Then, of course, as we hit 1994 and we really went into that major effort to get back to the Super Bowl, he was all over everything we did and why we did it and how we did it.

He would jump in, offer a suggestion or two, and offer to help out in any way he could. I'm convinced that there's not a thing that went on in that organization that he didn't somehow absorb. All along, he was preparing for the role of the leader he is now. Like all leaders, he has an innate desire to want to learn as well as an intellectual curiosity that causes him to get involved with anything that impacts his environment or what's happening around him.

I think he realized that someday, in the not-too-distant future, he was going to be a head coach in the NFL. I think he understood that he had to get a grip on what this was all about so that he could better deal with it. I think that he knew that was part of the educational process that a head coach in the 1990s had to go through.

In San Francisco, I felt as if he had coached every position on offense because he knew what everyone on offense was supposed to do. And I think he, in his own way, made sure that the men who were taking the field understood what they were supposed to do. He handled the meetings, and I understand he still handles the meetings in Denver. He knows what's going on in the locker room, he knows what's happening on the practice field, and he makes it his business to be certain that whoever represents his offense is a student of the game plan. That's his idea of preparing.

Now once he's done that, then I honestly think that explains the coolness he's able to maintain on game day, because he knows down deep inside he truly has done all he can do to win. Preparedness is what has enabled him to maintain the confidence and the stability and the even-temperedness that he demonstrates. The only other thing he could possibly do is to get out there and play the game itself.

11

TEAMING UP

WINNING IS NOT FOR THE SELFISH

No matter how isolated each of us might be in our jobs and our lives, there isn't a single one of us out there who doesn't live within the framework of some type of team. Your family is a team. So is your neighborhood. And your congregation. And, of course, your business.

The key is understanding how to make your team the best team. As the former great Green Bay Packers coach Vince Lombardi once said: "Individual commitment to a group effort—that's what makes a team work, a company work, a society work, a civilization work."

When it comes to teams and teamwork, so many of the winning principles are the people principles. How do you treat people? How do you deal with people? This book is laced with advice about that, but it is just as important to understand team concepts. Those who do will inevitably be more effective at helping themselves in business and in life.

It surprises me how many people fail to grasp the concept of teamwork. Why is it that each year in the NFL, the teams that win the most pick the lowest in the draft and the teams that lose the most pick the highest and yet, year after year, it seems as if the same teams are picking high and the same teams are picking low and nothing ever changes? You would think that eventually the teams that are poor would have better teams and improve quickly because they're picking better players. But that's hardly the case.

The teams that have good structure, good management, good coaches, good players, good sales forces, and good organization almost always find the way to win. Their expectations and their goals are so consistent, those teams find the way to win year in and year out. It is why every thread that goes into making up every team is so important.

You might be able to do it all, but you can't do it all by yourself.

As a former offensive coordinator and head coach who has had the privilege of being associated with some great offenses, we've scored some points through the years. Now, some more.

My fifteen-point plan to help you become a better team and teammate:

1. Teams Matter More Than Individuals

After our 8–8 finish during my first season as Broncos head coach, I didn't feel as if our Pro Bowl tight end Shannon Sharpe was putting the team first. If he didn't get the ball, he would go over to the bench and sulk. His lip would hang all the way down to his belt buckle. And I let him know.

"You're a one-dimensional guy, Shannon," I told him in our postseason meeting in my office. "You don't practice all the time, you're always getting nicked. I know how much you love all your catches, but from now on, we're going to spread the ball around. We're going to get it to other receivers for the good of the team.

"As for the running game, if you don't block, and if you don't become a complete football player, we can't run the ball and we can't win championships. It all comes from being unselfish. A team player.

"I know how much you love going to the Pro Bowl, but the feeling you get from playing in a Pro Bowl is nothing compared to winning a Super Bowl. There's nothing like putting that ring on your finger and knowing how important it is to put team first. When we get good is when you start taking as much pride in your blocking as your receiving."

The next season, Shannon blocked like an offensive lineman. Terrell Davis went from 1,117 rushing yards to 1,538. And our record went from 8–8 to 13–3. The season after that, blocking better than ever, Shannon discovered what it was like to win a Super Bowl and put a ring on his finger. And today, he is a much better blocker than people realize. The way he has blocked, combined with all his catches, should make him a slam-dunk for Pro Football's Hall of Fame.

Shannon and the rest of our players now have the attitude that no one is more important than the team. You can be the leading salesman, the top CEO, but if your team doesn't win, so what?

2. Every Job Is Important

To achieve greatness as an organization, every person must do his part. So often the head coach or quarterback gets too much credit when the trainers, the equipment people, and the secretaries deserve plenty, too.

There's no such thing as an unimportant job. Every job in your organization is the most important one and must be done as well as possible. I don't care if it's running back Terrell Davis playing every down of the game or safety George Coghill coming in for kickoff coverage, everyone must perform at a certain level.

If one person fails to do his job properly, then the whole organization suffers. With the Broncos, for example, even our groundskeeper, Ross Kurcab, does his job better than anyone in the business. If he didn't, then he might inadvertently leave a hole somewhere in the practice field that a player could step in, spraining his ankle, missing the game, and costing our team the chance of winning. But we try to make it so that there are no holes anywhere in our organization.

3. Treat Everyone with Respect

This is something as basic as arithmetic, yet not everyone does it. I try to treat people the way I would want to be treated myself. It's an excellent rule to go by. On our team everyone—not just the football players—is treated like a champion. It doesn't matter whether it is the janitor cleaning the hallways, the ball boy collecting the equipment, or the computer programmer designing a web page for the team. If you're the lowest-paid person in our organization, I'm going to treat you the same way I treated John Elway or Joe Montana or Steve Young.

4. Share Victories and Defeats

Our team knows that if we win, everybody gets recognition. If we don't, nobody does. That's why there can be no separation in your organization. You win as a team, you lose as a team. If we win 3–0, the offense knows the defense saved it, and it must prepare better. If we win 40–38, the defense knows the offense saved it, and it must prepare better. You cannot allow an offense-versus-defense, selling-versus-buying, us-versus-them antagonism to develop. If you stretch together, practice together, meet together, travel together, then you win together. As a team.

5. Accept Criticism

In 1995, during my first season as the Broncos head coach, our cornerback Ray Crockett sacked Chiefs quarterback Steve Bono, grabbed the ball from him, and raced down field all alone. When he got to about the 5-yard line, he began high-stepping and moonwalking and showboating, until finally, after spending a good three or four seconds straddling the goal line, he went into the end zone—not the kind of behavior I condone.

What made it even worse was that we lost that game, 20–17. He's dancing around and we're losing. The morning after our loss—strongly believing in resolving your differences promptly—I took aside Ray and explained my feelings.

"Number one, what you did is not fair to our football team," I told him. "There's a lot of things that can happen to you on the one-yard line. You could drop the ball. Somebody could strip it from you. Or we could be penalized before you cross that goal line, which would wipe out the touchdown. So our first thing, always, is to cross that goal line. Go into that end zone right away.

"Number two, you made a great play, and I'm really proud of you for it. But a guy like you who has a lot of class should show it on the field, too. That's not the way anyone on this team handles himself. That was demeaning to you and to our team. I'm surprised you didn't just get into the end zone and flip the ball to the official. Act like you've been there before."

"Coach," Ray told me, "you're right. It won't happen again."

During our first road game of the 1998 season at Oakland, Ray intercepted a key fourth-quarter pass. As he ran 80 yards upfield, toward the end zone, there was no one near him again. But this time, he crossed the goal line and politely flipped the ball to the official. He acted like it was no big deal, like he had been there before, which he had.

6. Keep the Boss Well Informed

In certain organizations, the head coach might say, "If anything happens, I don't want to know about it." Let me tell you right now, you don't win that way. To me, you've got to know. Whoever is in charge must know everything that goes on in his organization.

I tell our assistant coaches, "If you're being considered for a job opening and you want it, let me know. I might be able to help you get it." I understand the way this world works, that everyone wants a promotion, and assistant coaches want to be head coaches.

The week we were playing the New York Jets in the AFC championship game, our offensive coordinator, Gary Kubiak, came to me and asked if I thought he would be crazy to consider taking the head coaching job at the University of Colorado. I told him no, I thought it was a better job than fifteen NFL head coaching jobs, it could be a great opportunity. When he said it was something he was really interested in, I made a couple of phone calls.

The next day, we had Colorado athletic director Dick Tharp drive to our training complex and interview Gary in my office for two hours. I figured, Why have those guys meet in public, in some restaurant, where they can be readily recognized?

The interview went well, Gary was offered the job, but in the end—one day after we beat the Jets to go to the Super Bowl—he decided not to take it. He thanked them, wished them luck, and went back to his Super Bowl preparations.

Because Gary kept me well informed, our loyalty and trust had been even further strengthened. Gary now knows I'll do anything to help him get any job he wants, and I know that as long as he is in our organization, he will not let anything distract him from the job he has to get done.

7. Focus on Your Work Ethic, Not Others'

People are always evaluating other people. One person might be in the office at 5:00 A.M., two and a half hours before one of his co-workers comes in, and right away, he's got something against that guy because he feels he is working harder. Then, when there's some adversity, the early bird might think it's because other people are not working as hard.

I tell my people to consume themselves with being the best at their job. Some people can get done in ten hours what others can do in fifteen. One person might show up at 7:30 A.M., but he might have been up at 5:00 A.M., working from home. Or the guy might take his work home with him at night, putting in extra hours when others aren't.

You don't know what people do on their private time, nor can you be concerned about it. All you can be concerned about is what contribution you're making.

8. Allow for Differences in Lifestyle

Everybody has their own way of doing things. A perfect example is our linebackers coach, Frank Bush. Frank does a great job and he's very productive. When I walk into Frank's office, though, he'll have on headphones, listening to his favorite CDs while bopping all around to the music.

Every time I see it, I say to myself, "My God, if I were doing my work like that, I would lose my mind!" But that's Frank's method of concentration. So what if I need it so quiet I can hear the air conditioner turning on or shutting off? It works for him, and if it doesn't disrupt anyone else's work, then that's fine with me. Let the music play.

9. Be More Creative Than Predictable

Anyone who is too predictable plays right into his competitor's hands. If your competitor knows what you are going to do, he can obviously prepare for it and possibly stop you.

I'm still angry with myself for the way I handled a 4th-and-goal from the New York Jets' 1-yard line in the AFC Championship game. Before the game, I said, If we have a 4th-and-1, I'm going to run the ball, because I felt I had thrown it way too much in that situation. Jets defensive coordinator Bill Belichick knew I had. He was prepared for it. He had his players playing a solid, sound defense, ready for anything.

Then, when we got into that 4th-and-1 midway through the first quarter, what did I decide to do? Throw the ball. I figured we might as well keep on doing what we'd had success at. But Jets linebacker Mo Lewis batted down John Elway's pass, and I was furious at myself. I did something that I had planned not to do. I got caught up in the moment.

Because I became predictable, I lost that battle.

10. Let Go of Bad Ideas

Throughout the NFL drafts I've been through, I can't tell you how many times I've heard someone say, "This player is a good player, I like him, he's got strong character, the guy can run."

Then after we're with the player about a year, you know this guy can't play dead. Everyone knows it. But since you've invested so much time and effort in him, since you've put your stamp on his being hired and it's your reputation on the line, you say, "Let's keep him around an extra year."

Hey, you're not fooling anybody but yourself. A bad idea is a bad idea. Don't try to save it. Anybody who makes decisions is going to make mistakes. Just cut your losses and move on.

11. Employ Structure and Order

People say to me, How can you, at five-ten and 175 pounds, make these big guys do what you want? What makes them listen to you? Simple. Players thrive on organization and regimentation; anyone does. People, and particularly players, love to be coached, to be taught, to be disciplined, for one simple reason: They know their livelihood depends on it.

12. Reward Those Who Produce

What I tell our coaches is that our players must be productive. It's our job to find a way to bring it out of them.

I cannot tell you the number of knock-down, drag-it-out fights I had with Raiders owner Al Davis when I coached in Los Angeles. At wide receiver, I wanted to play Tim Brown and he wanted Willie Gault. Al loved Willie's speed, but he was dropping too many balls.

Now, I love Willie Gault; he's one of the classiest players I've ever coached. I went to bat for Tim Brown because in my opinion, he had outplayed Willie on a daily basis during practice. I could not look our team in the eye and say, "Tim is going to be on the bench and Willie is going to be the starter."

As usual, Al won. Willie started. But in the long run, Al just could not hold back Tim. He was producing too much. While Willie retired after the 1993 season, Tim went on to become one of the top receivers in the league, an annual Pro Bowl selection.

13. Find Different Ways to Motivate Your Employees

Do whatever you can. You'd be amazed at the little things, the seemingly silly ideas, that work.

Shortly after I became the Broncos coach, I instituted something called "Hat Day." If players won on Sunday, they would get to wear baseball hats rather than their football helmets to practice on Friday. It sounds like something little, but you'd be stunned. You would have thought I promised our players $1 million bonuses.

In the fourth quarter of games, I've actually heard our players yelling at each other, "C'mon! I'm not wearing a helmet to practice Friday!" They also tell free agents we've had visiting our complex, "You come here, it's Hat Day on Friday!"

The free agent gets a confused look on his face. "Hat Day?" he'll ask. "What's that?"

It's another and different way to motivate our team.

14. Keep Your Employees Fresh

Coming through the coaching ranks, I worked in programs where coaches asked their players to hit as hard as possible during practice. Many times, they were all beat up for the games. When I got to San Francisco, the 49ers would practice without pads and I couldn't understand it. But then the more I studied it, the more I realized it was a major contributing factor for their having the best November and December records in the history of football. Their bodies were less worn down and still capable of performing at a high level.

So during practice now, instead of having players hit each other, we have them work on drills that emphasize their speed, quickness, and explosion. We also ask our players to practice at the speed we play at on Sunday. That takes the place of contact—and, quite often, losing.

15. Protect Your System

When you're having success, members of your organization are invited to do speaking seminars and coaching clinics. And so many people like to tell other people how good they are, and how they managed to become the best, that the secrets of your system seep out.

You cannot offer elements to others. That's why I've never done an X's-and-O's football book, diagramming our plays. You'd have to beg, borrow, and steal to get at that. I would never do that to our team.

Now some might wonder, aren't you doing just that with this book? And my answer is, *Think Like a Champion* offers life's winning principles, not the intricacies of our X's and O's strategy. You still must figure out how to be the best in your field. Every job has its own variables and tricks, and I hope these pages provide you with the general steps that will work in business and life.

Now you just have to go out and apply them.

TOM JACKSON

Former Denver Broncos Linebacker and ESPN Football Analyst

There are so many things to be admired about Mike. The first thing that strikes me is the almost brutal honesty of the man. Some people would say that he doesn't say much, but I think when he says something it is that much more important. If you've ever listened to him talk to his team, as an example, the messages are clear, they're clean, and very well defined.

Mike has a tendency to treat everyone with an equal amount of respect. A lot of people say they do that, but Mike practices it. During the April [17–18] weekend of the 1999 NFL draft, when I was in Denver for ESPN, I sat in his war room and had a chance to see another side of Mike Shanahan.

Mike could run roughshod over the draft if he so chose. He has the decision-making power and he can direct his team in any way that he would like it to go. But he would make his pick by narrowing his choices down to two or three guys, then he would call all of his scouts and assistant coaches into a room and ask them to vote. Now I'm sure if the vote were close, Mike would have the ability to have the final say.

Mike said, "Let's see a show of hands for two guys." One of those guys was Tennessee linebacker Al Wilson. Al Wilson got the most votes. Al Wilson got chosen.

By doing this, Mike not only gives the people around him a sense of fair and obvious hands-on involvement, but he also makes them accountable for that kid's future and how he fits in with the organization.

Where did he learn that? I'm not sure. I think that the answer of, "Oh, he learned that in San Francisco" is a little too easy. I believe part of the character of the man is to respect other individuals, to respect people who work hard around him, and to make sure that he reciprocates in kind when you give your best to him. Then he's willing to give his best back.

I think that's immeasurable when you're in a business, any business, where you have to have a hands-on approach with people. But it's something that Mike has, and everybody recognizes it very easily. It's not difficult to see, it's just hard to find.

His team plays as a team. I think they have almost redefined what you can get out of group effort. The Glenn Cadrezes of the world, the Daniel Neils—not some of the stars of this football team—those people are now walking around with two rings and I think almost to a man they would tell you that it is in large part accountable to the fact that Mike Shanahan is the head coach of this football team.

When Shannon Sharpe gave his brother, Sterling, his Super Bowl ring and Mike replaced that ring unbeknownst to Shannon, I told people, "Mike did that because he wanted to do that." If he didn't do it, Shannon wouldn't have been expecting it, so it wouldn't have mattered. But since Mike did do it, what do you think the amount of dedication is now between Shannon and Shanahan? I think Shannon would run through a wall for him right now.

Mike understands not only the psychology of the game, but the psychology of human beings. He has the right touch, the right words, and, ultimately, the right feeling for his players.

One of the most poignant moments I've ever seen in a locker room—and I was in a lot of locker rooms over the course of fourteen years in the NFL and now twelve years with ESPN—came before Super Bowl XXXII. The Broncos were double-digit underdogs to the Green Bay Packers, and they were waiting on Coach Shanahan to give the pregame speech, knowing that it was going to be a defining moment for the day. This was going to carry the team.

I was in two Super Bowl locker rooms where I was playing and the coaches went on and on about a once-in-a-lifetime opportunity, and we can't let it pass us by, and we've got to get maximum effort, and they think we're not as good as they are. But Mike came in, and said just fifteen words: "Men, let's go out and show the world what kind of football team we've got." And he walked out the door. And that was it.

It did exactly what he knew it would to his team. It lifted them emotionally. It lifted their confidence, because they could see it in his face—I could see it in his face—that he couldn't wait to get out on that field and to do to Green Bay what he did.

The players said to me later on, "That's Mike." There wasn't anything else to say. He had prepared them to play. He had gotten them rested so they were physically ready. He had given them a game plan that they knew would work. And with those fifteen words, he gave them the confidence they needed to go out and ignore the fact that they were double-digit underdogs and feel like they actually should go out and dominate the Green Bay Packers.

It was as marvelous a moment as I've ever had in a locker room and as I told Mike later on, "I wasn't going to play a down, and I was ready to go hit somebody."

Mike Shanahan leaves nothing to chance when it comes to preparing his team to play. And his team knows that, his staff knows that, everyone around him knows that, and it translates into a winning attitude.

12

MAKING BREAKS
THE LUCKY FORMULA

It's always funny to me that people actually believe in lucky charms—not the cereal, the real thing. They wear lucky suits to business meetings, or drive a lucky way to work, or carry their lucky key chain hoping it provides the break they need.

This happens every day, everywhere. People here in Denver have come to believe that because we are 21–0 in the home navy blue uniforms we introduced and began wearing before the 1997 season, we have undisputed lucky uniforms. There were people who actually expressed some concern when we had to wear our white uniforms for Super Bowl XXXIII against Atlanta. But we were so prepared that if we had played in our pajamas, we still would have felt good about our chances.

For a while, my son, Kyle, honestly believed he was our team's good luck charm. From the time I took over as the Broncos head coach, we had never lost a game in which Kyle held my headset cords on our sideline. Then he missed the January 1997 playoff game against Jacksonville—a friend took him on a cruise during Christmas break—and we lost.

When the Broncos went to Super Bowl XXXII in San Diego against the Green Bay Packers, Kyle kiddingly threatened to hold out. My son joked that either I get him a hotel suite in San Diego, or he wasn't coming. Tough negotiator, my son. But he came, we conquered, and I saved our owner Pat Bowlen the added expense of another suite.

Last season, after Kyle enrolled at Duke and could not attend many of our games, a completely opposite streak started. Kyle missed our first thirteen games and we went undefeated without him. Then he attended our next two games, at New York against the Giants and in Miami against the Dolphins, and we lost both. And he actually came up to me, disturbed about this.

"Hey, Dad," Kyle told me, "I'm not lucky anymore. I shouldn't be on the sidelines any longer."

I told him, "You think you have that much control of our team that you being on the sidelines is the difference? I wish I could blame it on you. It's me not doing a good enough job preparing them for what they should be doing."

We went back to work, Kyle returned to the sidelines, and we got back to winning.

As crazy as it is, people don't only believe there are lucky charms. They believe there are lucky people. Everybody knows somebody they think is a lucky person. They are in your neighborhood, in your office, in your congregation. They are everywhere, these lucky people, aren't they? They're always managing to find just the way to be in the right place at the right time.

Hey, there are people out there who probably say the same thing about me. My family—knock on wood—is basically healthy. There have been no tragedies, none of the setbacks that can happen to anybody at any time. My wife, Peggy, doesn't have to work; she can remain at home and continue doing the fantastic job she has done raising our children. Kyle is entering his sophomore season as a wide receiver at Duke University, where he is on scholarship. Our daughter, Krystal, is entering her senior year of high school just outside of

Denver. With the strong influence Peggy has been able to exert, they've developed into great kids.

We live in a terrific city, in a nice neighborhood, with quiet streets and pretty homes and spacious back yards. Each day I get up for a job that I could not imagine being any better. Last season our team became only the sixth franchise in NFL history to win back-to-back Super Bowls, and this season we have a chance to become the first team ever to win three straight Super Bowls.

People say to me all the time, It's amazing! You've come a long way from a modest Franklin Park background, you're one of the two or three highest-paid coaches in the NFL, you have a wonderful life, you have to feel like the luckiest guy in the world.

And I do.

But let me also say this: there was next to no luck involved.

At least not the luck most people think of. To me, luck means capitalizing on your preparation, on your desire, on your work ethic, so that when opportunity arises you are able to recognize it and seize it.

The only luck there is is the luck you create for yourself. It comes in forms of good and bad. Good luck follows those who spend their time wisely, pursuing their goals constructively. Bad luck follows those who spend their time foolishly, waiting for their luck to change and their break to come.

Sooner or later the most successful people realize that luck does not propel you to greatness. You propel yourself there.

There were those that said Lady Luck was on our roster when we beat the Steelers in Pittsburgh in the 1997 AFC Championship game. With two minutes left in the game, with the ball on our own 15-yard line, and with our team facing a 3rd-and-6 while we were clinging to a 24–21 lead, John Elway screamed "All Thunder" in the huddle. Problem was, our tight end Shannon Sharpe could not hear the play call over the ear-splitting crowd noise.

As they broke the huddle, a confused and desperate Shannon yelled back to John. "WHAT WAS THE PLAY?"

"JUST GET OPEN!" John yelled back.

"Just get open?" Shannon told himself. "Okay."

On one of the biggest third down plays in franchise history, Shannon ran an eight-yard hitch pattern, bobbled one of John's bullet passes, and then thankfully reeled in the ball, the game, and the Super Bowl berth.

Luck? I guess you could say so. But I like to think that John and Shannon had worked together so much for so long, they knew how to read each other's minds like husband and wife. Plus, we had played well enough to have a three-point lead at that point. Our team—not the Steelers—had earned the right to go back to the Super Bowl.

That's how it works. The people who work the hardest always seem to be the luckiest. During the 1998 season, we were playing Jacksonville in October when our kicker Jason Elam tied the longstanding NFL record with an impossibly long 63-yard field goal. With four seconds remaining in the first half, before I sent Jason out onto the field, I pulled him aside first.

"Can you make it?" I asked him. But I never would have even asked him the question if I hadn't seen Jason kick 63-yard field goals ten different times during practice that season.

"I think I can get it there," Jason told me, and I felt his confidence.

Moments later, he did. He made the kick, and made it into the record books, tying the record that former New Orleans Saints kicker Tom Dempsey had set against the Detroit Lions twenty-eight years earlier.

Some said Jason was lucky his kick came in Denver's light air, at the end of the half when we had nothing to lose to try it. But the Broncos have been playing in Denver since 1960, and no one else had ever made a kick from anywhere near that distance before. Jason had practiced the kick, worked at it, and deserved it. We padded our lead to 27–10 to boot.

Based on my experience, I've worked up a little formula for luck: Preparation plus desire plus work ethic equals luck.

To me, when you're trying to judge personnel in any field, what you're really trying to do is eliminate your mistakes and decrease your chance for errors.

When we elect to draft a certain player, a lot of effort and research go into each of our decisions. As a coaching staff, we spend as much time as possible looking at game film of the top college players at each position.

Every coach looks at every player before we have our first draft meeting in March. Then, after each defensive coach has studied each available defensive player, our staff assembles three weeks before the draft and reviews the game film together. Two weeks before the draft, we do the same thing with the offensive coaches, studying every available offensive player. Then, in the last week, every coach and scout go over all the players together, one final tune-up before draft day. By the time we're done with our intensive film analysis, we've got a feeling about what's the right way to go.

Now, is it error free? No, nothing is. But by having scouts talking with players, position coaches studying players, coordinators supervising their decisions, and me overlooking everything, we have prepared ourselves to limit our mistakes.

Whether we're preparing for a game, for free agency, or for the NFL draft, we do our best not to leave anything to chance. That's the only way I believe in doing things. I like my chances when I don't leave anything to chance. But if you are going to leave something to chance?

Then chances are, you're not going to get what you want.

As it is, there are opportunities out there for each one of us. It's up to us to find them. Sometimes, if the circumstances you are working under are more difficult than your competitors', you just need to dig deeper to uncover the best opportunity available to you.

This is exactly what happened during my first NFL draft as the Broncos head coach in April 1995. The Broncos regime before me had traded its first-round pick to Atlanta for wide receiver Mike Pritchard, its second-round pick to Minnesota for offensive tackle Gary Zimmerman, and its third-round pick to Philadelphia for cornerback Ben Smith. Our first pick in my first draft as Broncos head coach was not scheduled to be until the fourth round. Not exactly the best circumstances to try to rebuild your team and make your mark.

I remember assembling our assistant coaches and scouts and telling them we had to spend more time than ever before studying game film of college prospects. For one full month, we had to forget about coaching football at mini-camps, forget about working with players one-on-one. We had to be film critics, and we had to find something special about somebody who was going to make the difference to our football team. That was our only choice.

Each assistant went to work, logging overtime hours. And one injury-prone running back, for a variety of reasons, kept standing out to our offensive coordinator, Gary Kubiak, and our running backs coach, Bobby Turner. The more film Gary and Bobby watched of the running back, the more they liked him. After seeing enough film, they began making phone calls and background checks.

First they called Texas A & M's offensive coordinator, Steve Ensminger, who had been Georgia's offensive coordinator for one season. A ringing endorsement there. Then they called Georgia quarterbacks coach Greg Davis, asking about the running back. Another ringing endorsement.

But Gary and Bobby were also thorough in their line of questions. Not only did they ask about the player's physical skills, they also asked about his personality traits. They asked whether the running back was a responsible person, whether he fit in well with teammates, whether he worked hard. And Steve and Greg gave Gary and Bobby all the answers they wanted, along with one other bit of advice.

If the Broncos—without a pick in any of the first three rounds—could find themselves a way to get this running back, they would be getting themselves a real steal.

Personally, due to a couple of reasons, I don't think very many people knew this running back when he was coming out. He missed a lot of playing time due to groin and hamstring injuries. And ever since Vince Dooley coached there, Georgia always has been a school that declined to open its practices to NFL scouts, something I remembered from my coaching days at Florida.

Now it just happened to be that we weren't even looking for a running back in that draft. We had just signed away free agent

Aaron Craver from the Miami Dolphins and we already had former second-round draft choice Glyn Milburn on our roster. Because of previous trades, we had only so many picks in the draft, and much more gaping holes than the one we had at running back.

But when we got to the sixth round of the draft and everybody who we thought could make our team already had been taken, we noticed the running back whom we scouted so well still sitting there. We had him ranked as a third-round talent and here we were in the sixth round, so we said, "Let's take a guy who has got a chance to make our team, even though he might not play a position of need."

And with the 196th pick of the 1995 draft—after 195 mistakes had been made—we selected Georgia running back Terrell Davis.

Turned out to be a pretty good decision. Terrell has gone on to win the Super Bowl XXXII's Most Valuable Player award and the National Football League's 1998 Most Valuable Player award, become only the fourth 2,000-yard single-season rusher in NFL history, and he now has a real shot at being the all-time best running back ever to play the game.

Now if we knew what he could do, we obviously would have taken him in the first round if we had a choice. But I don't think you really know what kind of player you have until someone actually comes into training camp. You've got projections and you've got ideas, but until a player actually comes in and shows what he can do, there are always those question marks about his talents. But the first day Terrell came in, we said, "This guy is going to be something special." And he has been.

Sure, there was a little luck involved there. But there were twenty-nine other teams that had a shot at him and didn't pull the trigger. We were lucky in that no one else saw his potential. But because we were thorough, we gave ourselves the advantage we needed.

A simple plan, carried through to the end, translated into the best luck we could have ever had.

Back in the summer of 1941, the great New York Yankees outfielder Joe DiMaggio strung together his still-record fifty-six-game hitting streak. Asked one day if there were any luck involved in his streak, DiMaggio shrugged.

"There has to be an element of luck to it," DiMaggio said. "But the one thing that sticks in my mind is that whenever I kept the streak alive with a scratch hit, I always came through in that same game with an honest hit that could not be questioned."

Everyone needs a break here or there. Sometimes the difference in landing a coveted job is simply who you know or being in the right place at the right time. But once you get your break, then the rest is up to you. Accomplish enough on your own and like the great DiMaggio, you too cannot be questioned.

TERRELL DAVIS

Denver Broncos Running Back

By now it has gotten pretty old, but there are people out there who still think the Broncos were lucky when they drafted me in the sixth round of the 1995 draft. I've been around Mike Shanahan long enough now to know that there wasn't too much luck involved.

Mike Shanahan has an eye for talent. He doesn't just look back at a person's stats and say, "Well this person can play," or "This person can't play." He watches film, he studies, he looks and sees if the person can do the little things right.

There are a lot of talented players out there who are not highly marketed when they're in college, but Mike has a knack for finding them. He's out there looking for those hard-working, blue-collar players. I was in that situation. No one thought highly of me. But it wasn't a pick out of the dark, like I thought at first. It's a credit to Mike that his coaches and scouts had their eyes on me.

Our whole team is built around people who have been late-round picks or players no one else wanted. Last season, when John [Elway] wasn't playing, we didn't have a single guy on our offense who was a first-round pick, yet we still led the AFC in offense.

Center Tom Nalen and tight end Shannon Sharpe were seventh-round picks, fullback Howard Griffith was a ninth-round pick, guard Mark Schlereth was a tenth-round pick, and offensive tackle Tony Jones and wide receiver Rod Smith were not even drafted. I could go on and on, listing guys whom Mike has gotten the most out of. Not all the players were guys Mike drafted, but so many of the players he has acquired were guys who weren't getting a lot of looks from other teams.

Is that lucky? Is it lucky we became only the second wild-card team in NFL history to win the Super Bowl, when we beat the Packers? That's not luck. Mike wouldn't expect anything less from us.

He makes us all feel like first-round picks who are capable of anything. Mike has a way of making people feel important. From top to bottom, the way he runs the organization is first-class. It's the little things that go a long way, like giving each player his own hotel room on the road and free Spectravision movies when we're on road trips. He makes it as comfortable for his players as possible, so that when you're out there playing, you're playing for him.

The other thing that contributes to Mike's success is his temperament. I've never seen Mike get excited. He is intense no matter what the situation is, I don't care what kind of game we're playing or how many games we've won. With Mike, it's work, work, work, and he's never really content with winning one or winning two championships. I don't think he'd be content with winning even six or seven championships.

Right after we won the Super Bowl, I could already see Mike's mind working on next year. I swear, it was like, "Congratulations, men, now let's go for three." And everyone in that locker room felt the same way.

To us, it felt like we had just won a regular-season road game, not the world championship. There was no hugging and kissing, no wild and crazy celebrating. That's a reflection of Mike's temperament. When you look at him and you don't see him being all crazy after you've won a championship, it carries over to the team.

On our team, winning surprises nobody. With Mike, he wants the best, demands the best, and gets it.

13

RISK TAKING

SHOOTING THE ROLL OF YOUR LIFE

While planning for success, there are various steps to implement. Once you believe in yourself, establish your goals, learn from the best, prepare to win, and pay attention to detail, you have the option of rolling the dice.

Few things are more exhilarating than going for it on fourth down, coming dangerously close to being shot down and escaping without being hit. Or going to Las Vegas and playing blackjack and keeping the money the casinos bank on pickpocketing from you.

Judging from this, you might call me a gambler. And I am. But any time I gamble, I try to play the odds—in football, in Vegas, in life.

If I thought I were taking a crazy risk, I wouldn't do it. That is why I take risks only after I have studied and analyzed a situation. I know that if I have prepared myself, then the taking of the risk will usually pay its rewards. And once I've committed myself, I don't worry about my decision. If it works, people will probably say I'm fearless, I'm bold. If it doesn't, then at least I know the decision was thoroughly thought through.

For me, taking risks and playing the odds are a chance to separate yourself from the pack.

Last December, when we were playing Kansas City and trying to extend our winning streak to twelve games, the Chiefs held a three-point lead on us less than midway through the final quarter. We faced a 3rd-and-1 at the Chiefs' 24-yard line. The safe call would have been to send running back Terrell Davis into the middle of the field, over the pile, for 1 yard and the first down, then, if the run failed, kicking the tying field goal.

And that was my first thought. But during a timeout, as I thought about the defensive tendencies of the Chiefs that I had studied, I decided to change the call to a pass to our tight end Shannon Sharpe. Is that taking a risk? Yeah. Up until that point, the Chiefs had been playing man-to-man coverage on Shannon, with zone coverage behind him, shutting him down without a single catch all day. But what kind of risk was it really?

Our percentage of kicking a field goal from 40 yards or beyond was 73 percent. Our percentage of making a first down on 4th-and-inches was 90 percent. And typically on 4th-and-1 plays, our film analysis showed that the Chiefs loved to play ten of their eleven defenders on the line of scrimmage, guarding heavily against the run, meaning we would have had the opportunity for a home run on fourth down.

So on third down, essentially with a free play, we ran a play-action handoff fake to Terrell that worked to perfection. The Chiefs were thinking run. Their safeties charged the line. And in the secondary, Shannon got open and reeled in a game-winning 24-yard touchdown pass. And when somebody expects you to go conservative and you put them away with a kill shot, it is completely demoralizing—which is what you are aiming for.

After the win, as I was buttoning my navy-blue suit, Shannon came up to me, shook my hand, and said, "Great call, Mike." But actually, it wasn't. It was, based on the odds, simply the safest call.

The call might have looked dangerous, but the work and preparation made it easy.

This is how you should try to make as many of your decisions as possible. Very carefully, you should weigh the percentages of any action you consider taking. When the odds are in your favor, then you know it is time go for the throat and put your competition away. When the odds are not in your favor, it is time to scale back your operation and wait for the right moment to strike.

Yet sooner or later the time comes for everyone. The questions are whether you recognize it, and whether you're ready for it.

When I go to Las Vegas—and I try to go once or twice a year—I know the percentages aren't with me, so I'm not going to get carried away with how much I gamble. When you keep cutting your own throat—in anything—eventually you run out of blood.

Now I love the games, the competition of them, but I know in the long run that I have to lose at the tables. There's a reason they build all those nice buildings out in Vegas—because they understand the percentages, as well as the betting man's hope for glory. Yet each weekend, thousands of hotel rooms in Vegas are stuffed full with people thinking they're going to be lucky.

What Vegas is doing is entertaining—and stealing. They know just what they are going to make on the slot machines every day. If you're not careful, you can go out there driving a nice $30,000 car and come home riding in the back of a million-dollar Greyhound bus. So when I go, I know the odds of each game and make sure my play is smart. I don't get carried away until the odds are with me. When they are, wherever they are, you can roll the dice wisely.

And if you roll them wisely, it could turn out to be the roll of your life.

When it comes to taking risks in your personal or business affairs, the lesson is always the same: Success does not visit those who straddle the fence of indecision. It visits those who evaluate their decisions thoroughly, weigh the pros and cons, and then find the answers if not in the percentages then in a rational and well-thoughtout manner.

Shortly after Super Bowl XXIX in January 1995, while I was the San Francisco 49ers offensive coordinator, I had to make a career-altering decision. At the time, the Denver Broncos had offered me their head coaching job, needing an answer as soon as possible. This was a scenario the 49ers had anticipated, what with all the speculation around the league and in the newspapers.

Before the Broncos' offer even came in, the 49ers made it as difficult as possible for me to leave. In an effort to entice me to stick around for the next season and a whole bunch of them in the future, San Francisco took the radical step of guaranteeing me, in the form of a behind-the-scenes contract, the job as successor to 49ers head coach George Seifert whenever he decided to step down.

As a further inducement, the 49ers also agreed to match the $1-plus million salary the Broncos were offering for me to remain as San Francisco's offensive coordinator, making me what would have been the highest-paid coordinator in football history. The deal also came with the promise that once I did become the 49ers head coach, they would tear up my contract and redo it, making it an even greater and more alluring salary.

A seductive offer, to say the least.

Making it even tougher to pass up, George Seifert then pulled me aside to recommend that I take the offer and stay in San Francisco rather than leaving for Denver. I remember it distinctly. George told me he wasn't planning on coaching a whole lot longer—a statement that was substantiated when he left the 49ers before the 1997 season—and that he would rather not have to train another offensive coordinator.

And there was a part of me that wanted to stay with an organization as rich in tradition as San Francisco's. But frankly, the setup concerned me. I felt that eventually, even though only the 49ers' inner sanctum knew about the proposed arrangement, word would get out about why I was remaining as an offensive coordinator in San Francisco when I had the opportunity to become a head coach in Denver.

In my mind, this would have undermined George indirectly, even though he truly wanted me to stay. There would have been people in the organization who knew I already had been anointed the next head coach, and where would their loyalties have been? With George or with me?

That would have been a divisive force working against what had been, up until that time, over the past two decades, a model organization. It easily could have separated the team. And I didn't know that that would be an environment in which we could continue winning, no matter how well positioned and stable our coaching staff was.

The other element that entered my decision was that I wanted the challenge of doing something no one else had ever done, and that was coaching the Denver Broncos to their first Super Bowl win. San Francisco already had won five Super Bowls; Denver hadn't won any. Had I remained in San Francisco, we would have just been trying to feed the monster. In Denver, we had the chance to create one.

Now, did leaving an established organization in San Francisco for a sub-.500 team in Denver represent a risk? Of course. A lot of people told me I was completely crazy, both financially and professionally, to go to Denver when I was guaranteed a job at San Francisco. But once Denver's offer came in, I never wavered.

Quite often, unlike being in a football game or in a Vegas casino, you will be unable to calculate the percentages for the risk you are considering. That's fine. There's no need to get upset about that, as it happens on a regular basis. When it does, then it's time to resort to your other method for helping you decide when to take risks.

Trusting your instincts.

For my first head coaching interview with Al Davis and the Raiders in 1988, all I cared about hearing was how much money they were willing to pay. My instincts told me not to take the job, even though it was paying more money than I had ever made. Yet I ignored my inner voice and took the job.

For my second head coaching interview—my first with Pat Bowlen and the Broncos in 1993—I was that much better prepared. This time, salary was the least of my worries. When Pat and I sat down, I had a list of things I wanted answered. I wanted to know what my budget would be for hiring assistant coaches, how much money I could spend on the free agent market, who would have the final decisions on personnel matters, who would determine who was on our football team. The answers were not exactly what I wanted to hear.

So, as difficult as it was to do, I turned down the Broncos' first head-coaching offer. It was hard, being that the Broncos job was the dream job. But unlike when I accepted the Raiders job in Los Angeles, this time I trusted my instincts.

More often than not, your gut is going to be right. Every now and then it might turn out to be wrong, but not usually. Back in the early 1960s, Ted Turner took over a billboard company that was deeply in debt. Even though some said he was making a mistake, his instincts told him otherwise. He borrowed heavily and saved the company.

Once the billboards began producing money, he used it to buy a small local TV station, which he turned into TBS. Then, in 1980, when there were even more doubters, Turner played another educated hunch. He started a twenty-four-hour news channel, CNN. The news business was forever changed.

A risk? Sure. But as Turner has joked, there were a lot of people telling Columbus that sailing to the west was a bad idea, too.

Ultimately, taking smart risks comes from preparation and confidence. With those two elements, regardless of the inherent problems in a given situation, you can make anything work.

Look at the Minnesota Vikings. During the April 1998 draft, with the twenty-first overall pick, they pulled the trigger on the checkered past and immense talents of wide receiver Randy Moss, who now is threatening to become one of the all-time greats.

Without even realizing it, there are risks you take each and every day. You invest your time, your energy, and your money in your job and your family, all with the hope that the return on your investment is realized one day. And some risks obviously are more significant than others. During our 1999 off-season, we decided to pursue one, and only one, free agent: Kansas City cornerback Dale Carter.

Many considered this to be an explosive risk. As talented a player as Dale is, there were questions about his character. In 1993, Dale was arrested twice—one time for driving under the influence, the other for carrying a concealed weapon. In 1994, he was arrested for assault. And in 1995, he served fifteen days in jail and seventy-five days in home detention for violating his probation from his 1993 weapons conviction.

But we studied Dale's background. We talked to the people close to him. We interviewed the people who knew him extremely well. I'm guessing that twenty other people's opinions were factored into our decision about whether to pursue him.

During the 1998 off-season, I remember bumping into then-Kansas City defensive coordinator Gunther Cunningham. Knowing that Dale's contract would be up one year later, I asked Gunther what he thought about Dale. Gunther praised the guy, and I remembered the recommendation for a full year.

Then, just before Dale hit the free agent market, I talked with Rams assistant coach Al Saunders, who left his job as receivers coach with Kansas City after the 1998 season. Al had one message for me: Sign him as quick as you can.

Even former Chief Joe Montana, whom I knew from the one season we spent together in San Francisco in 1992 before he was traded to Kansas City, endorsed Dale. Joe said Dale might just be the best athlete he had ever played with. And when I watched film of Dale, I could not believe how talented he was. The only cornerback in the league who might be better than Dale is Deion Sanders, whom I worked with in San Francisco during the 1994 season.

(And Deion, by the way, took a risk coming to San Francisco at an annual salary of $700,000. He could have gotten four or five times that with other teams, but he felt San Francisco gave him the best shot to win a Super Bowl. He was right.)

So our decision basically became a no decision. The odds, I believed, were greatly in our favor. Less than two weeks after the free agent signing period kicked off, we landed Dale with a 4-year, $22.8 million contract that included a $7.8 million signing bonus.

Of course, there were second-guessers. There always are. And that prevents people from taking many of the risks that they should. Not willing to expose themselves to doubters, some take a more conservative approach and prevent themselves from accomplishing great things.

If you take chances and they don't work, you're a bum. But if they work, instead of everybody saying, "He's nuts!," they say, "He's so open-minded, he attacks!" So you can go from being one of the most innovative play-callers and the guy who's willing to take chances to being a bum faster than you could lose $100 in Vegas.

But if you are prepared, you have to be willing to not care what other people say. The late Dick Howser, who managed the 1985 World Series champion Kansas City Royals, was once asked if he ever second-guessed himself.

"No," he replied firmly.

"Why not?"

"Because," he said, "nobody has ever proved to me that the second guess would have worked."

Pretty hard to second-guess that.

One of the most second-guessed areas, where so many risks are taken, is the NFL draft. Each April, some of the picks baffle me, but none more so than at quarterback. Of all the players and positions available in the draft, quarterback is easily the worst evaluated.

It's amazing to me how some teams will take a quarterback in the first round when you have him ranked as a fifth-round talent. I've seen players we've had ranked as fourth-round picks go in the top ten. It is why I love to play the odds with quarterbacks.

During the 1993 draft, while I was still with the 49ers, we had Michigan's Elvis Grbac rated as the draft's second-best quarterback, behind Washington State's Drew Bledsoe and just ahead of Notre Dame's Rick Mirer and Washington's Mark Brunell. San Francisco was loaded at quarterback and I made my pitch for

Elvis in the fourth round, the fifth round, the sixth round and the seventh—which gives you an idea of how much pull I had there. The 49ers did not take Elvis until the eighth round.

Elvis went on to help the 49ers get to Super Bowl XXIX and later, as a free agent, left San Francisco to become the starting quarterback in Kansas City. But that draft left me with something more than a strong relationship with Elvis. It left me with the idea that if you see a quarterback in the third, fourth, or fifth round whom you feel is a second-round talent, why wait to take him? The odds are with you.

And when you base your risks on previous experiences—knowing what works and what won't—the better you become at judging the right time to strike.

Now, it's always better to have full control over all possible variables. But sometimes, as is only natural, you won't. Inevitably, uncontrollable things will occur. A ball will bounce a certain and uninvited way. But the way I figure it is, if you don't drop the ball, you only have to worry about 50 percent of its bounces instead of 100 percent.

Then the odds begin working for you, instead of against you.

SHANNON SHARPE

Denver Broncos Tight End

Everybody says Mike Shanahan likes to bungee-jump and race cars and jump off cliffs and ride motorcycles. I haven't seen that side of him. Yet, on the field, I've never seen anybody take as many chances as Mike. It doesn't matter when, where, or how.

You can be on the 1-yard line, 99 yards to go, and you think, "The guy's going to run the ball a couple of times into the line, give the punter some room, and punt the ball away." That's not Mike's philosophy. If he's on the 1-yard line, Mike might play-action fake your ass and throw the ball deep down the middle of the field. Or he might call a triple reverse. Whatever the play, it wouldn't surprise me.

When we played the Chiefs on Monday Night Football [in November 1998], Mike called for a naked bootleg. I didn't really think he would let Bubby Brister run that play so early in the game. But he did, and that was really the play that set the tone for the game because we came out and on the third play of the game, Mike said, "Let's use it." I said, "Why run this play?" But everybody went left and Bubby went right. Touchdown.

That's why Mike's successful, because no one else is willing to take those risks. I read a quote somewhere that said, "A genius sees something that no one else sees and he hits it." Well, that's Mike. Mike says, "I believe that I can get my team to do this. Now, they don't see it right away, but they will." Because I don't see things as Mike sees them at first. But once you start going, then you're like, "Okay, now I see why I did this."

The greatest trick Mike ever pulled was convincing us that we are invincible once we step on the field. We actually and really and truly believe that when we step on that field, we're going to win the ball game. It's not, "Well, if we play well, we might win the ball game." We feel if we play our C game, we're going to beat 85 percent of the teams in this league. If we play our B game, it's going to be 98 percent. If we play our A game, we can't be beaten on a Sunday or a Saturday or a Monday or a Friday or a Thursday or Tuesday or a Wednesday or in a cornfield or in a Super Bowl.

That's because of the way Mike gets us to approach games: Mike says, whether you're in there for ten plays for a preseason game or you play every play in the Super Bowl, you give me everything you got. That's all I ask for. That's all. And that's the way we approach it.

To me, being successful is awfully easy because there are so few people who challenge you at the top. Everybody just wants to get by, but that's not how Mike wants to do it. Mike wants to be the best, and to be the best requires you to take risks that another person wouldn't take or has taken and failed. But the thing about Mike is, he knows what he can and can't do. He's not impulsive.

See, there are two types of gamblers. There are impulsive gamblers and there are instinctively methodical gamblers. Mike is not impulsive. He's not rash. Everything is calculated. He is methodical in his approach. He is very careful, he is very drawn out. He watches more film than we ever do. He not only reviews films with us, but if you ever go into his office, he's watching even more film. I'm sure his wife thinks he's crazy because he probably studies film when he goes home, too.

Still, it's not like we have any problem talking to him. I've been around coaches at many levels that said, "If you have a problem with something, come talk to me and we'll get it done." And if you went to go talk to them, they'd say, "We're sorry, we just can't do that." That's not Mike. I have never ever been to Mike—and it might be the smallest thing with Mike—and been denied.

I'll say, "Can we get orange juice instead of water for breakfast?" Or, "Can we get egg whites instead of just regular scrambled eggs?" Or, "Could we get french toast instead of pancakes or two free movies on the road instead of one?" Whatever it is, he comes through for his employees.

It's kind of like a trickle-down effect. If you see your top dog, your CEO, your president go that extra mile, more times than not your employees are going to be willing to go that extra mile for you. That's what he's convinced us about.

He's the best, and because of that we're the best.

14

PERSEVERING

FALLING HARD, BOUNCING HIGH

Throughout history, all winners have encountered crushing defeats before claiming ultimate victory. In the end, they persevered, not allowing their defeats to keep them down or hold them back.

One of my favorite examples is one of our nation's greatest leaders, Abraham Lincoln. He was born into poverty, with the decks stacked against him. Twice he failed in business, contributing to the nervous breakdown he suffered in 1841. Later he lost two elections for Congress, in 1843 and 1848, two elections for the Senate, in 1855 and 1858, and one election for Vice President, in 1856.

It would have been enough to make an average man quit. But Lincoln was not your average man. He did not dwell on his failures. "The path was worn and slippery," Lincoln said after losing one of his Senate races. "My foot slipped from under me. But I recovered and said to myself, 'It's a slip and not a fall.' "

Finally, in 1860, after proving that character is built through defeats an individual is forced to overcome, Lincoln was elected President of the United States. Who knows where we'd be today if he'd given up? Who can imagine the resolution of the Civil War without Lincoln?

Some of the obstacles Lincoln faced more than a century ago were not altogether different from the ones you face today. People feel, as they are experiencing them, that their rough times will last forever. Nothing lasts forever. But if you stick with your plan, if you believe you will overcome, eventually you will.

It's okay to fail every now and then. Everyone does. But do not fail due to lack of effort; that is a mistake worse than any other.

A bend in the road is not the end of the road—unless you fail to make the turn. The ability to fight on in spite of difficulties is almost always rewarded. Perseverance pays.

Successful people don't give up, because they have that one dream, that final goal, that ultimate ambition they've chased since they were a little kid. They know deep down that unless they give it their best shot, they'll never be satisfied with themselves.

And they also realize something else.

The harder you fall, the higher you bounce.

Raiders owner Al Davis was the first person ever to fire me from a job. And I knew it was coming well before it happened.

Back in the summer of 1989, as my wife and I were sitting around our house in Palos Verdes, California, I told her, "You watch, right after our fourth game of the season, Al will get rid of me. For sure." Why? Because the following week we were traveling to the biggest media market in the world, New York. We had a *Monday Night Football* game against the New York Jets. If Al fired me then, he would receive even more publicity than usual.

And there were problems brewing almost from the outset. When I first left the Broncos offensive coordinator job to accept the Raiders head coaching job in 1988, I asked to bring aboard my own assistant coaches. Al declined my request. He asked me to spend a year working with the loyal assistants he already had in place, to at least give them a chance before making a decision about their futures. I wasn't happy about it—no head coach would be—but I agreed.

After I arrived there, during the season, it became clear that several of the Raiders long-time assistants did not like the fact that their new head coach had come from outside the organization, rather than within it. They were unhappy. Our approaches were different. They were used to practices in which we ran fifty or so plays at a slow-paced style. I wanted to run eighty plays in rapid-fire succession.

Not to say they were wrong and I was right. But for the success of the team—and based on my experiences with other successful teams—I felt it was imperative for everyone to be on the same page. And as a head coach, that page should be mine. So at the end of the season, after I had given the opportunities that Al demanded, I dismissed defensive backs coach Willie Brown, quarterbacks coach Tom Walsh, and linebackers coach Charlie Sumner.

From that point on, I thought things would be new and improved. But life has a way of being unpredictable. A few days later, without consulting me, Al hired them all back. Now I knew the power struggle was on. Unfortunately, it was one-sided. Al had all the power and I had all the struggle.

I knew that if we didn't get off to a good start in the 1989 season—and I was thinking 3–1, minimum—I was walking the plank. Sure enough, on October 2, 1989, the morning after we dropped our third game in a row, a 24–20 home loss to Seattle that brought our record to 1–3, Al walked into my office. Now, he never got to the office before 11:30 A.M. On this morning, he was there at 9:00 A.M., so I knew something was going down. It was my job.

"Mike," he told me, "I'm going to make a change."

My prediction to Peggy had come true. The office I was sitting in now belonged to Art Shell, who was being promoted from offensive line to head coach. The one thing that I asked Al before I left the office for the last time was that he honor the year and nine months I had remaining on my contract. He agreed—with one provision.

"As long as you don't go back to the Broncos," Al told me.

As long as I went anywhere else — San Diego, Seattle, or even back to the college ranks—he would pay me the money I had remaining on my three-year deal. But if I went to the Broncos, Al vowed I never would see the money.

Now, you don't ever want to create or perpetuate any adversarial situations in your business. You want to try to limit your enemies. Which is why, as politely as I could, I pointed out to Al that I had a contract with his signature on it.

"I don't care about the contract," he told me. "It'll cost you more money to try to get your money back through lawyer's fees. Just don't go to Denver."

That was his last message to me.

During the final drive from the Raiders training facility in El Segundo, California, to my home in Palos Verdes, I was in shock. It was the first time I'd been fired. It was gut-check time, and I was feeling horribly inadequate. It was real tough to face that I hadn't accomplished what I had set out to do.

When I took the Raiders job at the age of thirty-five, I had extreme reservations about it. My honest gut feeling at that time was not to go. I just didn't feel comfortable. But everybody told me I should go, that head coaching jobs are tough to come by. Rather than researching the job more extensively, though, or ensuring that my demands were met in writing before I took office, I took the job. I made the decision to do it at 100 miles per hour.

People still say to me, "Well, Al Davis didn't give you a chance. You weren't able to hire your own coaches, you were forced to run a different system. He gave you three years on your contract but only allowed you to fulfill one year and four games of it." To me, all those things are excuses. When I accepted the job, I accepted it as is. Ultimately, it was my fault. And at all times, no matter the circumstances, you must know who is responsible—you.

It's like I've told my son, Kyle: "You're going to disagree with the decisions that people make. It doesn't matter if they are right or wrong. You can't get down on yourself. You've just got to keep on working and convince the people who matter that you're the best." If you think you are deprived of an opportunity, instead of getting mad at that person, try something else. But you can't become negative. You've got to keep working and learning from your mistakes, not duplicating them.

Before you can enjoy life, you must accept this basic tenet: Life isn't fair. It becomes fair only when you realize it is unfair. Once you know it isn't, you're on a more level playing field, and you're better prepared for it.

After the Raiders fired me, I didn't complain. That would have been useless. The situation was done, there was nothing I could do about it anymore. The only thing I knew I could do now was to work just as hard and even harder to overcome this and whatever damage it might have done to my reputation.

The question now was, where would I go? Who would give me a chance to bounce up after my hard fall? When I walked in my front door about an hour after Al had given me my walking papers, I had my answer. My wife Peggy was on the telephone with Denver Broncos owner Pat Bowlen.

Despite Al's warning, I would be returning to Denver.

Tom Hanks does not win an Oscar every year, Wolfgang Puck does not prepare perfect pizza every time, Mark McGwire does not homer at every at bat. No matter how much success you have had, you must confront unwelcome failures. But losing can reveal a lot about people. It forces you to analyze yourself and see how you can improve. And the biggest mistakes you can make, in my mind, are not trying to turn negatives into positives.

Successful people treat crushing defeats as learning experiences, nothing more than temporary setbacks that make them stronger, not weaker. They understand that struggle and strength go together.

Think about it. The more you struggle to bench-press 200 pounds, the more likely you'll eventually lift that weight; the more you struggle to run a six-minute mile, the more likely you are to break that mark.

I'm sure you've heard that adversity builds character and strength. These are, in my mind, the two most important components of persevering.

During the 1996 season, we built more character and strength than even I could bear. In our opening playoff game, following a 13–3 record and what was then the best regular season in franchise history, Jacksonville beat us 30–27 in Denver at Mile High Stadium. It was one of the biggest upsets in NFL playoff history. The Jaguars, an expansion team, were only in their second year of existence. We didn't take them as seriously as we should have, and we paid dearly for it. That game still sticks in my craw, even today.

I remember that the night of that loss, after I got home, it felt like there was a death in the family. But something compelled me to call each one of our coaches and tell them what a great job they did. I called a number of players and did the same. I knew how down everybody was. It was the bleakest night of my career and the franchise's history.

I told our running back Terrell Davis, "Life is full of opportunities, and sometimes you take advantage of them and sometimes you don't. But that's not what's most important. It's how you respond to those misfortunes that really determines the character of a person."

Throughout the off-season, I reviewed our preparation the week prior to the Jacksonville game—the way I had addressed the team, the way we had designed our game plan, the manner in which we had implemented it. No matter how many times I broke it down, my realization was the same: I did not prepare the team as well as I should have. We did not approach the game with the sense of urgency you need to win. Period.

When you have a failure, it is important to give your opposition the most credit. They beat you. But you also must remember the feeling, and remember how miserable it is, so you can ask yourself, as I repeatedly did, "What can you do to make sure this doesn't ever happen again?"

I was hardly the only one consumed with our wasted opportunity and using it as motivation to come back even stronger and better. Our linebacker Bill Romanowski actually hung a picture of Jaguars quarterback Mark Brunell in the entrance of his workout room. Each morning when he walked into that room he would gaze at the player who ruined his year.

The next season, I knew we had to set loftier goals. In 1996, the season we lost to Jacksonville, I had challenged our team to win the AFC West title and home field advantage in the AFC. I never mentioned anything beyond that. Well, we ended up meeting our goals on December 1 and, subconsciously, strange as it might sound, we felt content with that.

When we reported to training camp in 1997, I had a different message. I told our team I didn't care whether we were division champs or wild cards. We just wanted to get into the playoffs and win enough games to be world champions. The goals were set higher. And the results were more favorable.

At the start of that season's playoffs, we vented a year's worth of rage during our opening-round 42–17 playoff win over Jacksonville. That began our journey to our first Super Bowl victory, during which I learned a valuable lesson: You can't keep winning unless you know how much you hate losing.

The other notable and invaluable thing about struggling and persevering is that they make you appreciate the good times all the more. Every adversity carries with it the seed of its equivalent or even greater benefit.

Look at John Elway. People forget that he never went to a bowl game when he quarterbacked Stanford. Never. When he was drafted, everybody said, "He's a great quarterback, but he has never taken his team to a championship." But John believed, he never quit, he kept on working. He got the Broncos to the Super Bowl three times, but he never won it. Many thought that was it, that he never would have another chance to win again.

But John never lost confidence. And the rest is history. The man left the game a champion. But it would not have been as sweet had he first not tasted the bitter.

After all these years, I'd like to think I have persevered. And now that I have, I would like to formally address the money Al still owes me from my Raiders contract. In 1990, in Los Angeles, the

NFL conducted an internal hearing and issued a ruling in my favor. NFL commissioner Paul Tagliabue determined that Al still owes me the $250,000 he refused to pay me if I took a job with the Broncos, which I did the week after he fired me.

It now has been ten years and I still haven't seen a penny of it.

So here's my proposal. I don't need the money anymore, but others sure do. I am now willing to forget about the money Al still owes me if he simply will donate it to the Oakland Unified School District. It is a standing offer, one he has declined to comply with since I first made the proposal in November of the 1997 season.

But here it is, once again. He took me to school, and now I am willing to do the same for him. The Oakland Unified School District could use the money more than Al.

For them, persevering sure would become a whole lot easier with another $350,000—that's including interest—in their coffers.

MARCUS ALLEN

Former Raiders and Kansas City Chiefs Running Back and Current CBS Football Analyst

I have a sense that Mike feels he was destined to be where he is right now. What he went through with the Raiders when we were there together was a necessary growth process. It was a loss that strengthened his resolve. Adversity like that makes you focus on what you want to accomplish. It makes you appreciate success that much more.

My running backs coach in Kansas City, Jimmy Raye, used to tell me, "If you work on being a good person, those same principles will make you a good athlete and help you to be the best you can possibly be—in all facets of life." Mike exemplifies that in his teachings.

I learned a lot about the game from him. The essence of Mike is his passion. He loves his job, he loves his family, he loves his players and the people around him, and I don't think he's afraid to express it. It shows. You can see how his players respond to him.

Mike and I always had a bond. I've always pulled for Mike and I think he's always pulled for me. In Los Angeles, he was obviously handcuffed. I saw the situation that he was in, and he knew my situation. [Author's note: Allen and Raiders owner Al Davis repeatedly clashed over, among a variety of things, philosophies and playing time. Davis relegated Allen to the bench, and when the running back became a free agent in 1993, he left the Raiders and signed with the division rival Chiefs.]

Through all the years that Mike and I played against each other, that support continued. Every time we played against each other, we'd make eye contact across the field during the National Anthem, then wave to each other. It was a flick of the wrist, a very subtle gesture. It was a sign that I'm thinking about you, you're thinking about me, but now we've got to go to war. Out of respect for each other, though, the feeling that we have is much greater than the outcome of this game. That was something about Mike that I always greatly admired and respected.

It wasn't just me, either. When we were with the Raiders, we knew there was a vertical arrangement with management. With Mike, though, it felt horizontal, where everybody was on the same level, whether it was the groundskeeper, the secretary, or the star player. Everybody was treated with the utmost respect. I think that was part of the formula for success. When you show people you respect them and care for them, they'll die for you, and Mike knows that.

With the Raiders we used to have the roach coach, a truck that would come by and feed us lunch. But Mike started the tradition of a buffet at lunch for his players and coaches. It doesn't seem like much, but it was monumental. Guys really respected that, and you could see they really wanted to work for Mike.

But in L.A., the situation was out of everyone's control. That team really didn't prosper like it should have. Mike had a philosophy and he was hired to implement it. And like always with the Raiders, the other philosophy wins out. It was sort of foolish. You hire a coach, let him coach. Why bring him in? The reason he wasn't successful was there was just too much opposition from the obvious. That's the only reason. Given time, the Raiders could have done exactly what the Broncos are doing now.

It's interesting to me because you hear coaches say all the time, "I don't want to be liked, I just want to be respected." Believe me, if players like you and respect you they'll do just about anything for you. I always use Vince Lombardi as a measuring stick. Players initially didn't like him because he pushed so hard. But in the end they loved him, because he brought out the best in everybody.

That's what Mike's doing now, bringing out the best in his team. Now, in my mind, you have to look at Mike as one of the all-time greats. There might be some opposition from people because he's young, but his record speaks for itself. It's undeniable.

15

SUCCEEDING
WHEN GOOD ISN'T GOOD ENOUGH

In every mutual fund prospectus is one line in fine print that you'd miss if you didn't look closely. As small as it is, though, it is extremely important.

The line: "Past performance is no guarantee of future success."

This is a caveat well worth remembering. As I often remind my players, it's easier to get to the top than to stay there.

Who would have ever thought that Gulf Oil, once a giant in the industry, would disappear? Or that Pan Am, a beacon in the airlines industry, would go belly-up? Or that Boston Market, a young-upstart successful company, would have to declare bankruptcy so soon?

Our business landscape is littered with such examples. It is why, on the first day of our spring 1998 minicamp, I assembled our team and informed them that success could be tougher to battle than any competitor we would face. I challenged them to be better than we had been when we won Super Bowl XXXII. I told them we had the foundation and the nucleus not only to be the best team in the game, but to be the best team *ever* to play the game.

Bold? Yeah. But I meant it and believed it. The way I figured it was, someone had to be the best team ever. Why not us? But I told them that for us to be the best team ever, the standard for our practices had to be so high, we couldn't ever falter, even when no one but us was watching. And if you have to do the work anyway, why not exert maximum effort?

With our team, I wanted to make sure we didn't let down one bit. Our players didn't. Knowing that we had to work even harder than we did the season before, thirty-eight players attended every one of our off-season workout programs. And not surprisingly, thirteen games into our season, we were on pace to do what I asked, and expected, of them. We were a perfect 13–0. Our run through the competition and toward the record books was right on schedule.

But then, all of a sudden, we stubbed our toe against history and the New York Giants and Miami Dolphins. We lost back-to-back games. They would turn out to be the only games we lost during 1998. In the end, we could not say we were the best NFL team ever. But after we beat the Falcons in the Super Bowl, we could say we were the best NFL team in 1998.

Moments after our victory, as our team huddled inside our locker room at Miami's Pro Player Stadium, I announced to them: "Off-season workouts start tomorrow. Because we're going for three!"

I was facetious when I said tomorrow, but I wanted to send the message that this isn't over. It never is. In the race to success, there is no finish line. It constantly outdistances us.

Our players obviously were listening. When I walked downstairs from my office to our locker room on the April day we commenced our 1999 off-season training program—which forty players attended—there were two white signs mysteriously thumbtacked to the bulletin board outside our locker room. Each player who walked in or out of our locker room had to see the quotes.

The first, a quote from a former Brooklyn law school professor named William M. Winans, said: "Not doing more than average is what keeps the average down."

The second, a quote from Winston Churchill, said: "This is no time for ease and comfort. It is the time to dare and endure."

This season we dare and endure to become the first NFL team ever to win three straight Super Bowls. It is an obvious challenge, one I need not even mention to our team. It is every bit as alluring—maybe even more so—as becoming the best NFL team ever. And it is within our reach.

Of course, we will be without our quarterback and leader, John Elway. As I've said, John wasn't just a great quarterback, he was a great presence. When he was around, we knew he would find a way to win. Yet the mindset of our team must continue to be that if a guy goes down, whether it is to injury or retirement, no one can prevent us from winning.

Outside our locker room, there are doubters. But as a competitor, and as a football team, when someone says, "Now you can't do it because you've lost a guy," that should inspire and motivate you. What do you mean, you can't do something? Why can't you? Champions thrive on such challenges. And they excel at finding ways to see the limits stretched.

We all know it's going to be harder to win without John; everyone does. And our schedule—which includes games against the Miami Dolphins, the Minnesota Vikings, the New York Jets, the Green Bay Packers, the Jacksonville Jaguars, the Tampa Bay Buccaneers, the New England Patriots, the Detroit Lions, and the AFC West—is the toughest one this franchise has ever had.

But our players are hungry men. Even though success steals some people's incentive, ours remains strong. Because I really believe that after you win a championship, after you know what it's like to be the best in your field and understand how much fun winning truly is, anything less eats at your gut.

Once you win, your problems might just be getting started. Not only are you fighting the enemy, you're also fighting human nature.

Once you've reached the pinnacle, human nature wants you to feel relaxed and relieved. But the time when everybody is patting you on the back and telling you how good you are is actually the time when your job becomes even more difficult.

To beat complacency, you cannot win with the status quo, simply doing what you did in the past. We went 14–2 last season, and there's a reason we lost two games. We weren't good enough down the stretch. We lost our edge. In future seasons, we cannot allow the same thing to happen.

You never can let up and believe you can turn it on when you have to. Any feelings of self-satisfaction, cockiness, or arrogance will cause you to lose respect for your opponent. Once that happens, you're in trouble.

You cannot let down in preparation, conditioning, or psychological readiness. You must prepare as though your job is on the line, which it is every day. Nothing lasts forever. Things can be going fine and then, before you know it, it all can be taken away. That's one of the things that motivates me to keep working hard with little letup. If you lose that edge—particularly in coaching—very often you lose your job.

It's like I tell our players: people don't worry about what you've done in the past. They want to see what you're doing now. Is it fun to put in all those hours preparing for the next day or the next month or the next season? Is it fun poring over videotape after videotape of the 350 college prospects for each draft? Wouldn't it be easier just to look at fifteen prospects and just make a snap decision? Sure it would. But at some point later on, you would suffer.

Look at former Broncos wide receiver Ricky Nattiel, whom I recruited out of Newberry High School in Newberry, Florida. After the Broncos selected him in the first round of the 1987 draft, Ricky was the only guy in good enough shape to run ten straight 40-yard dashes—with only a 20-second rest in between each—in under five seconds each.

But in 1989, we went to the Super Bowl, where along with Vance Johnson and Mark Jackson, Ricky got all kinds of attention for being one of the "Three Amigos." Along came fame and fortune—and trouble. That off-season, Ricky felt good about himself. He stopped showing up at our off-season training program. He didn't train the same way he had. Soon enough, even though he was a great athlete with great speed, the competition caught up to him. Three seasons later, Ricky was out of the league.

To beat complacency, you cannot let outside interests—such as TV appearances or autograph signing shows, for which our players are paid anywhere from $10,000 to $50,000—detract from your primary job. In our case, football has to come first, and other professional opportunities second.

You cannot have financial dealings that compromise and distract from your concentration. You cannot worry about other people, whether they are on your team or someone else's, are making. If you perform as well as you prepare to, there will be more money for everyone.

A perfect example is offensive tackle Harry Swayne, who started for our team last season. Two off-seasons ago, no one even wanted Harry. We gave him a chance, along with a two-year, $1 million contract. Then, during the 1998 off-season, the Baltimore Ravens signed him to a four-year, $13.2 million contract and called him their most significant off-season acquisition.

You think Harry, as nice a player as he is, would have gotten that money if he didn't start for a successful team and perform at a high level? If the job is done right, the rewards come for everyone.

Now, I'm not saying you can't enjoy your success; you can. But a lot of people will go to work and answer congratulatory telephone calls most of the day. The time to enjoy it is away from work, perhaps when you are with your family and friends, when you can reminisce about your accomplishments without any distractions.

My first chance to revel in our 1998 success did not come until almost three weeks after our Super Bowl win, when I left Denver to go to the annual college scouting combine in Indianapolis. In my briefcase, I packed a videotape of Super Bowl XXXIII. One night in Indianapolis, instead of watching game film of the college players. I inserted the tape into the VCR. I sat back, relaxed, and, in the solitude of my hotel room, enjoyed it while I could. That, I know, will not always be the case. Prosperity does not always last.

Look, as much as Broncos fans would rather not hear it, the day is going to come when we're going to have to make some big-time changes to our team. I don't want to set off the warning bells and screaming sirens, but too many guys are going to be making too much money and with the salary cap the way it is, we are not going to be able to afford them all. Our team will have to be torn apart.

That kind of thing happens all the time to successful football teams; the Cowboys and 49ers went through it. It just hasn't happened in Denver yet because we were fortunate enough to have everybody under contract through the 2000 season. But sooner or later those contracts are going to be up, players are going to have new opportunities, and we might be forced to play with younger players who must perform at a championship level.

In our field, everyone has a different definition of success. Some teams think it's making the playoffs, others think it's winning a playoff game. Deep down, our mindset is that unless we win the Super Bowl, our season has been a failure. Our philosophy is that we don't care how good we are, we're going to get better. We fully understand, as well we should, that past performance is no guarantee of future success.

No one stays at the same level. No one. You either get better or you get worse. And raising the bar is something the world's most successful people, throughout time, have understood.

After writing his first and second symphonies, Ludwig van Beethoven continued on, writing a third. After sculpting "David," Michelangelo continued on, painting the Sistine Chapel ceiling. After painting "The Last Supper," Leonardo da Vinci continued on, mustering the strength to paint the most famous woman of the art world, Mona Lisa. And rather than calling it a career after penning *Romeo and Juliet,* William Shakespeare continued on, writing *Hamlet.*

So as you see, greatness can produce sequels.

Now I guess we'll see if the 1999 Broncos can come up with a masterpiece of our own.

BARRY SWITZER

Former Head Coach of the Oklahoma Sooners and Dallas Cowboys

Back in 1975–76, when Coach Mike was on my staff and we won the national championship, we would have these great parties at my house. Alumni would come, my coaching staff would come. It was fantastic.

When Mike and his fiancée Peggy showed up, they would not only bring one girl, they would not only bring two, but they would bring three or even four sometimes. Yeah, Mike always made it interesting. Every week, I'd say, "So, Coach Mike, which sorority are you and Peggy bringing to the house this week?"

And he knows his football, too. When Mike came to us, he was a wishbone quarterback at Eastern Illinois, and we used his understanding of it for our own wishbone offense. We won thirty-eight games in a row and two national championships. We had a great run while he was here.

Mike's an excellent coach. He was here, and he was everywhere he's been. He's the same coach he was when he was with the Raiders and the same coach he was as an assistant with the 49ers, and when he was an assistant with the Broncos. He was a hell of a coach at Oklahoma, and in Florida, and in Minnesota. But like anything, you get more experience as you go along. Innovations change and you adapt, and that's what he has done. He has become more refined.

And I know he's an offensive coach, but it's always comical to me when I hear people say, "Well, he's an offensive coach or he's a defensive coach." Let me tell you, you coach this game, you've got to know both sides of the ball. Mike is a total coach, watching and understanding everything going on around him. He's young, he's got a lot of time left, and he's only going to do more great things.

A lot of coaches have similar attributes. But what makes the difference between the good ones and the great ones are the intangibles, the personalities, whether you're fortunate enough to be surrounded by good coaches and players. And Mike has been smart enough to put together an excellent system with some great talent there. That's key.

I think Mike would be honest and admit there are no gurus out there, but there are damn good football coaches who know how to line them up and how to orchestrate. And the ones who have the better talent usually are the ones who are going to win.

I'm smart enough to know the reason I won is because we were talented. I had better talent than most people. It wasn't that Barry Switzer was smarter than Tom Osborne. We just had more talent than everybody else. We kept that going, we recruited consistently every year, and we had some good people.

But think about this. Not only was Mike on my staff at Oklahoma, but so was Jimmy Johnson. Me, Jimmy Johnson, and Mike Shanahan. Between the three of us, we've won five Super Bowls. That's a pretty amazing stat. I'd say the University of Oklahoma is probably the only school that has ever had three coaches win five Super Bowls.

Now that Mike has won two Super Bowls in a row, I love it. I'm so thrilled for him. And you know what I like about it? The guy's still a good guy. And that's the only thing I look at a guy for. It's how he carries it, how he handles his success. That's the most important thing to me.

When I started out in the business, I had one coach tell me, "Son, it's not how you handle losing, it's how you handle winning. That's the most important thing you can learn in the game." And that is so important because in this game, humility is only seven days away. You better know that and understand that.

And that, most of all, is what has impressed me about Coach Mike. He has handled success like the champion he is.

16

BALANCING

JUGGLING THE PROFESSIONAL AND THE PERSONAL

If somebody were to show me a job where you only have to work nine to five, five days a week, to advance to the top of your field, I would be the first to apply. But as far as I know, there is nothing out there like that. The fact is, to advance to the top of your field takes time, and it inevitably has an impact on other areas of your life.

How to judiciously divide your time between work, family, and pleasure is one of the most difficult issues you face. Just take a look at the successful people you know. I'm sure you will find that some have jobs that provide riches, but seem to spend little time at home. Others are more family-oriented, but they may not have the affluent lifestyle of some CEOs. There are any number of degrees of difference between these two examples, and few have it all.

As a child, I was keenly aware that my dad would always get home early enough to spend plenty of time with our family. He was an electrician, with six kids, and my mom was a housewife. At no point in my childhood did I ever feel as though I were missing out on anything—ever.

But as I grew up and thought about my future, I told myself I wouldn't be content with my parents' lifestyle. I wanted more. I knew that when the time came, I wanted to provide my family with a nicer car, a nicer house, a nicer lifestyle. I also knew that to achieve these dreams I would have to devote more time to my work and less to my family than my father did.

I've seen my career as a means to that end. Putting in the work to ensure job security—and to keep my family comfortable—is a priority for me. But people can interpret this in different ways. Take my sister, Joyce, a lawyer in Chicago. She does not like working long hours. Barring some unusual, out-of-the-ordinary circumstance, she refuses to work any longer than nine to five.

At first, I really didn't understand it. I would say to her, "That's fine, but you're not going to become the top lawyer working those hours. You're going to be a middle-of-the-pack lawyer." Yet she would say she didn't care.

As she explained, her life is not about trying to be the top lawyer in the firm. Spending time with her family, doing little things for them before she goes to work and after she gets home, is more important than becoming the next F. Lee Bailey. The more I heard, the more admiration I had for her. Joyce knew exactly what she wanted to do.

And when you think about it, what it really comes down to is this.

Balance is a choice that only you can make.

Just as there must be a balance between running and passing on game days, there should be one between living and working every day.

With me, as I was climbing through the coaching ranks, it used to be that I could not take off more than one week at a time. Even when I was vacationing rather than working, I felt like I was cheating somebody. My mindset was always, Sorry, Peggy, sorry, kids, got to get back to work. I would hardly take any time off.

Then, when I got to San Francisco, as I was sacrificing my time and my life for the 49ers, they left me with no other choice. Sometime in June, about six weeks before training camp kicked off, they shut down and locked up their offices. For one full month. I was like, "Holy cow!" How are you supposed to get ahead when everyone else is working and you're not? I had never seen anything like that before in the NFL.

But what I underestimated was the power of escaping. It was therapeutic. After the organization's imposed month-long vacation, I had had enough golf, enough happy hours, enough free time to last for a year. I came back to work rejuvenated. I was fired up. I was ready to go. Rather than taking a week off and saying, "Oh, that was so nice, I wish I had a little more time," I was able to jump back into my job with a better perspective than I had during any other season.

In our profession, just as it is in any demanding field, it is imperative to get away. The great coaches and entrepreneurs always have been well-rounded people who see other parts of the world. Otherwise, it's more difficult to last over a three- or four-year time frame. If work is the only thing you do all the time, and you have nothing to look forward to outside it, you are looking for trouble. Burn out could find you before success.

While you're still trying to get where you want, clear out your calendars. Designate some free time. In our organization, right after we return from the Super Bowl, we try to make it easy for everyone. Our employees receive a six-month calendar spelling out every day they need to work and every day they can take off. They know their itineraries in February, so they can begin making vacation plans for June, as well as their days off in March, April, and May.

Our employees work as hard as possible while they are in the office. They also know that if they don't get their jobs done in the allotted time, they then have to cut into their vacation time. Amazing how productive people can be when they know their vacation time is riding on it.

The reason I hand out our itineraries so early is because of what I learned in the past. All the things that I once hated about being an assistant I try not to make my coaches do. We don't sit in hour-and-a-half meetings and just talk. I value their time and my own too much for that.

If we have a staff meeting, there's a purpose to it. I succinctly tell them what I need, and then it's over. Then everyone can get back to their previously designated responsibilities. And when those are completed, they can go play golf, go see their family, go do whatever it is that makes them happy.

I try to do whatever I can to provide the balance my employees' needs. It used to bother me to no end when a head coach would walk into my office at 4:00 P.M. on a Thursday afternoon in May and tell me I could be off the next day for a three-day weekend. Inside, they thought I was thinking, "Oh, thanks! Thank you! You're such a good boss!" when what I really was thinking was, "Why didn't you let me know this a week or month ago when I could have set up a weekend getaway for my family?"

Over the years, it bothered me so much that during my first year with the 49ers, I finally said to George Seifert, my head coach in San Francisco, "You think next year you could mark down a couple of Fridays in advance so we could plan a couple of three-day weekends?" George thought about it, liked the idea and went right along with it.

Every now and then, I'll even take an off-season vacation when people would least expect it. Three weeks before our 1999 draft, I gave my coaching staff one full week off. During that time, my wife, daughter, and I went to Los Cabos, Mexico, for some fun in the sun.

Most coaches around the league were in their offices, studying as much film of college prospects as they could. But I felt that our staff had worked hard enough in advance. Now, if we were not totally prepared as the draft got closer, I never would have done it. But we organized it to where we had studied so much film, conducted so many interviews, done so much research, that we could take a little break before the draft.

When we got back into the office the first Monday in April, our coaches had a little extra sunburn on their face and a little extra bounce in their step. And I couldn't have been more pleased with the players we picked.

Maybe the least appreciated part of balance, the area so few people talk about, is emotional balance. As you get older, and as you gain experience, you also gain a better perspective. Without even thinking about it, you take the highs and lows more in stride. You know there's going to be plenty of both during your lifetime. There will be good times and bad times, time to work and time to play. It's all part of life's great balancing act.

I remember back when we won the national championship at Eastern Illinois in 1978, I was celebrating like the kid I was. I was practically doing flips. I was just so excited and I remember the euphoria, and I really got caught up in it. But I understand why I did.

When you're young, you're just hoping to win. As you get older and you learn how to prepare better, you expect it.

You should also have something you enjoy doing outside your job. Hobbies and leisure activities are mini-vacations, little breaks you give yourself to take your mind off of work.

For myself, I pursue some out-of-the-ordinary activities. Some people like to read, others sit on the beach. Me? I could never. I don't mind sitting down for thirty minutes, but after a while, I just get too restless. I need to be as active as possible. It's so bad, my wife thinks I'm some kind of Evel Knievel with a whistle.

But I think acting a little like a kid on your free time can help keep you young. During another one of our trips to Los Cabos, I spent about 45 minutes catching air, hang-gliding 1,000 feet above the water. There was another time when I dove from a sixty-foot cliff into the Caribbean. During a family vacation in Las Vegas, I went over to the NASCAR track and got one car up to 160 miles per hour.

And then there was the family vacation, shortly after we moved back to Denver in 1995, when we went to Cancun, Mexico, and I took my son, Kyle, and my daughter, Krystal, bungee-jumping. They wanted to do it with or without me. So I said, "Well, if you guys are going to do it and something ever happened to you, I'd feel horrible, so I've got to do it first." Off I went, doing a flip on my first-ever bungee-jump.

My wife was none too happy that I jumped or flipped. But then, she's not real happy about a lot of my immature behavior. What bothered her most was when I bought a Harley-Davidson. I had always wanted one, but I said I would not get one as long as my son was around to drive it. I was afraid that when I was out of town he might take it for a ride. So when he left for Duke, my bike moved in.

Peggy was upset because she thought I should have learned my lesson back in the spring of 1971. Shortly after I had returned home to Franklin Park, Illinois, from my sophomore year at Eastern Illinois, my buddy Mickey Bertini and I decided to drive to downtown Chicago. Rather than taking the "'el"—Chicago's trains are the popular form of mass transit—we elected to take my Kawasaki 500.

"Okay if I drive it?" Mickey asked me.

"Go ahead," I said, handing him the keys.

We were off, zooming through the streets. Everything was going great until we entered a major intersection and a car made a sharp, fast, and illegal left-hand turn.

Head on into my bike.

I was thrown 110 feet across the street onto the sidewalk. Mickey lay in the street, bloodied. I limped to a pay phone and called an ambulance. A short time later, the ambulance showed up and took away Mickey. But thirty minutes after they arrived at the hospital, Mickey was pronounced dead.

His death was a difficult thing to deal with. And I couldn't help but think that if I had been the one driving, I'd have been the one who was dead. That's why Peggy cannot fathom why I would want another motorcycle.

But to me, it's a little like the high-wire walker Karl Wallenda, who at the age of seventy went back up in the sky, on the wire, after two members of his family already had fallen to their deaths. Asked why he would walk above the masses in the sky again, Wallenda said, "To be on the wire is life. The rest is waiting."

• • •

Family situations are vital. Do not ever hesitate to request special consideration when serious situations arise.

During the 1998 season, our special teams coach Rick Dennison came to me and said, "My son's in a big performance, can I go watch him?" I didn't say, "Stay here." I said, "Go, otherwise you'll miss it." Rick went to watch his son sing in the chorus and then returned to work, in time to complete his assignments.

My family knows that during the season, breaking away for me is next to impossible. The 100-hour work weeks are just too demanding. But my family, as supportive as they are, helps me find the balance I need.

They understand my long hours, and to try to make up for it, we maximize the time we do have together. We try to do what we can when we can. We eat dinner together every Thursday night during the season, and Peggy and I have date night every Friday night.

With Kyle, I missed only two of his high school football games. Now that he's a wide receiver at Duke, I cannot go watch him every weekend, but if the Broncos happen to have a bye weekend and Duke is playing, I'll head down to North Carolina to watch my son.

But even when I can't see him, Kyle's play does not go unnoticed. I have our video department tape the game off our satellite feed and I watch every down of every one of Kyle's games. He'll ask me for an honest opinion of what I think, and I'll tell him. Sometimes he tells me I'm too honest.

Krystal has her own extracurricular activities in field hockey and horse shows, and she's a champion of her own. In the summer of 1998, she won the Reserve National Championship at the youth nationals in Oklahoma City with her horse Hokus Pokus, an Arabian mare.

Fortunately I saw her win the championship, but during the season, I don't get to see a lot of her horse shows. She understands that I have a time-consuming job, and if I could be there I would and when I can, I am.

Would I like to be there all the time, for her and Kyle and Peggy? No question. But when I work, I work. When I'm home, I try to be completely focused on my family. It is the most balanced, and simple, advice I could offer.

Be where you're at.

AL MICHAELS

ABC Play-by-Play Broadcaster

I've met a lot of very well-prepared, intelligent people in my lifetime, not just in football circles, but corporate executives—people who have been tremendously successful and winners in whatever field they're in. But of all these people, Mike Shanahan has always stood out in that he seems to have another life as well.

I know a lot of very driven people who have had tremendous success but are absolutely consumed by what they do, and their occupation becomes the only thing in their lives that matters to them. But in all the years I've known Mike—and we first got to know each other when he was the Raiders head coach [in 1988–89]—I've always seen a tremendous balance with him.

After the [1999] Pro Bowl, my wife, Linda, and I had dinner with Mike and his wife, Peggy. The table was set up where Linda was sitting next to him, and Peggy was on the other side, and across from Mike were John Elway and his wife, Janet. It was a noisy restaurant, so you were sort of locked into whoever you were sitting next to or across from and obviously Mike has spent enough of his life talking to John. So Linda and Mike spent most of the night in conversation.

My wife said that it was so enjoyable. Mike talked almost not at all about himself, not at all about football, but was into everything else. He was very interested in what she had to say. She was very impressed with his range of knowledge about other issues, about how interested he was in other things, and I said, "You know, that's exactly the way I've always thought of Mike."

I've talked to enough other coaches who didn't know anything abut an impeachment process or world situation that's happening during the football season. They're not even aware of names that are in the news constantly. Mike's not that way. He is up on everything truly important that is happening in the world.

He also seems to have some semblance of a sense of humor, no matter how critical the situation is. I'm not talking about when a game gets extremely tense or there's a real crisis surrounding the team. I'm just talking in general terms as the season has gone on and all the times we've met with Mike and no matter what adversity he's facing at a particular time, he's looking for a little bit of a laugh or a chuckle to take the edge off.

His mood is so even-keeled all the time, at least externally. God knows what demons might possess him inside that we don't see. But I think Mike is smart enough to know that the highs can't be too high and the lows can't be too low because you have to keep coming back and doing the same thing each season. I think that's good for his mental and physical health, and also good for his team. They know what to expect.

Mike is a guy who has to spend an inordinate amount of time doing what he does. You can't accomplish what Mike has without putting your heart and soul and an incalculable number of hours into it. And yet he seems to always have it in perspective.

I would imagine that in time having perspective helps avoid the pitfalls that many very driven people fall into, where all their happiness depends on their jobs because there is nothing else in their lives. It's a tremendous trait, and I admire Mike for it because it makes him even better at what he does.

He's into everything but he's not consumed with himself. I'm beginning to see this around the league. I think some of the younger coaches have some of the Mike tendencies in various ways. There's a part of Pittsburgh coach Bill Cowher like that, even though Cowher can look as if he's far more intense than Mike. But there's a part of Bill that knows he's got to get away from it, he has to have other things in his life. And I think it's the only way these days that a coach can get through it. Otherwise, everybody will become like Dick Vermeil was in Philadelphia and like all these guys are after X number of years. They just kill themselves.

It's critical for them personally to get away, but also in Mike's case, he's able to combine the balance that he has in his life with a tremendous football mind. It's the kind of thing that separates him from a lot of coaches.

POSTGAME TALK

One of the keys to happiness is having dreams. One of the keys to success is making them come true.

Back in the spring of 1994 when my son, Kyle, was in the eighth grade, he had to run the mile for the high school he was scheduled to attend the following fall. When he got back home, I asked him how he did. Not good, he answered. He finished twenty-fourth, with a time of 7:48.

"What was the best time?" I asked.

"A five-fifty-one," he said. "Boy, I wish I could run like that."

There it was again, rearing its ugly head, The Wish Syndrome I despise, wishing for something rather than planning to do it.

"Well," I told Kyle, "I can guarantee you one thing. If you do what I ask you to do for the next six weeks, and not any more than one hour and fifteen minutes a day, five days a week, I can guarantee you that you will win the mile. Do I have the commitment?"

"Yes!" Kyle said.

Well, the first thing we did was break down his training methods, which were a study in misspent energy. He was going out and running one mile at a time, working hard as so many of us do, but he was working ineffectively. He didn't even realize it.

So I prescribed a new plan for him. Altering his training methods, I had him run 40-yard dashes, 100-yard dashes, 200-yard dashes, smaller incremental distances leading up to a mile. He did it five days a week, one hour and fifteen minutes a day, for six straight weeks. And the next time he ran that mile, he dropped his time to a 5:46. He went from twenty-fourth place to first.

It meant so much for him to win the mile, and it should have. The harder the road, the more gratification there is at the end of it. If something is easy, you can't appreciate it as much. But if you eye a challenge and say, "Hey, maybe I am in over my head, but I am going to make a commitment to get this accomplished," there is no better feeling than applying yourself and pulling it off.

As you see, it's not where you come from. It's where you end up.

After Kyle won the mile, all of a sudden I could see the light go on his mind that—wow!—if I can accomplish this, what *can't* I do? His attitude improved, and he became more confident in himself. He also became more likely to succeed in anything he wanted to do. His grades in math and English improved, and I could see he was putting more effort into things he might not have attempted, or might have given up on earlier.

This is the way we all should approach life. As the late great Green Bay Packers coach Vince Lombardi once said, "Your quality of life is in direct proportion to your commitment to excellence."

It's not one thing you do that gives you a chance to be the best. It's everything. But what separates the winner from the also-ran is the commitment. Are you committed? I hope that by now you are, and I believe if you carefully consider the suggestions I have offered you in this book, you can plan your success.

Let's quickly reexamine the sixteen components of my lifetime plan for bringing out the best in you and helping you build success one victory at a time..

- **Preparing**—This, as much as anything else, is a must. If you are prepared for every possible contingency, you will win. But if you fail to prepare, you prepare to fail.

- **Sacrificing**—No sacrifice is too great for the achievement of your ultimate goals.
- **Learning**—Study and learn from the mistakes and successes of the best in your business.
- **Detailing**—Take care of the small details and the big picture will take care of itself.
- **Understanding**—Know your strengths and weaknesses, your likes and dislikes; maximize your strengths, minimize your weaknesses; and pursue your passion.
- **Setting Goals**—Goals give shape to your dreams and provide you with the necessary steps to achieve them.
- **Believing**—Be positive, believe in yourself, and nothing can stop you.
- **Competing**—Understanding your competition is key to defeating them.
- **Communicating**—Communication solidifies relationships and reduces misunderstandings.
- **Leading**—Accepting the responsibility of leadership includes picking great leaders in your organization and giving them the power to inspire.
- **Teaming Up**—Good teamwork elevates everyone's play and helps them achieve their individual—and collective—goal of winning it all.
- **Making Breaks**—Preparation plus desire plus work ethic ensures that you are going to be luckier than most.
- **Taking Risks**—Calculated risks help define you in a culture of mediocrity.
- **Persevering**—Without adversity, there would be no challenges; without challenges, no greatness.
- **Succeeding**—Maintaining success is as important as achieving it.
- **Balancing**—Balancing your personal and professional lives allows each of them to thrive.

It also is important to point out the importance of finishing the job. The most successful people I know are great finishers. They don't do the job right for three-quarters of the time or seventh-eighths. They do it from start to finish.

In a sense, the football world is a unique world. But the more I am asked to lecture at various businesses I admire, the more I talk to the various entrepreneurs I respect, the more I realize that every business values the same components: believing, competing, communicating, persevering, sacrificing, making it happen.

Not too long ago, Nike asked me to deliver a lecture on leadership and winning values to its employees in Portland, Oregon. And after I finished my presentation, I rode back to the airport with Nike's NFL marketing manager, Bob Giraldi, who told me about his company's business policy.

Among other things, Bob said Nike constantly was striving to integrate principles of long-term effectiveness into all its business decisions; seek business partnerships with suppliers who value the same things; educate its employees, customers, and business partners to support their goals; partner with experts and organizations that contribute to its knowledge; and monitor, measure, and report progress.

Doesn't every organization and every employee in every field want to do the same? The difference, in my mind, is all the people who really stick to their plan. A lot of people talk about the success they want and the principles involved, but not as many have the unbridled passion, the burning desire, and the tremendous work ethic necessary to follow through and make it happen.

It always surprises me how many people claim they want to be the best, but then go ahead and leave their offices at four o'clock in the afternoon. Often, these are the same people who don't work weekends. Now, I'm not denigrating their desire for leisure or family time. That's their decision and if that's what they want to balance their life, I think that's commendable.

But no one can be the best—and I don't care what the personal or professional situation is—focusing nine to five, five days a week. It's simply impossible. Life does not work that way.

Somewhere out there, while you're taking time for a weekend getaway or a long bicycle ride, persistent people are willing to work the longer hours that you're not. They are working nights, weekends, whatever it takes to get ahead. You think Bill Gates works nine to five? You think he shuts it down early when every day, depending on what his stock does, he could win or lose about a billion dollars? He probably works as hard, if not harder, than he ever has.

Being the best takes an enormous commitment and an intense focus. How do you think Joe Montana and John Elway became the best? When they were out there performing, nothing else mattered to them. They had no idea there were people in the stands watching them, booing them, cheering them. They didn't know any of that. All they knew was the job they had to do, and nothing could stop them. They were playing in their own world, with laser intensity. But you do not need Montana's or Elway's superior talents to make it to the top of your field. Other qualities can help take you there.

As an offensive coordinator at Florida in the early 1980s, we had five quarterbacks on full scholarship and four were heavily recruited—Wayne Peace, Mark Massey, Roger Sibbald, and Dale Dorminey. The fifth, Larry Keefe, was the worst athlete of the crew.

Yet rather than resign himself to defeat, Larry did everything he could to compete for a starting position. When it became obvious he would not start, he asked to be moved to defense. We tried him at strong safety, at linebacker, at defensive end, but there was no area in which Larry could make an impact. He refused to give up, though, and ended up playing special teams—kickoff returns and punts. He played well enough that he was elected our special teams captain for a number of games.

After I left the University of Florida for the NFL, I checked in with some former Gator friends to see how Larry was doing. He had finished school at Florida with almost straight As. He then went on to Florida law school, where he did quite well. And his first job was with maybe the top firm in the state, Shackleford-Farrior in Tampa.

Today, Larry is a successful attorney at Anchors, Foster, McGinnis and Keefe in his hometown of Fort Walton Beach,

Florida. It is no surprise to me. Anyone who gives their best, and has a plan for how to do it, more often than not is rewarded for it.

And on the road to where you want to end up, there is another nugget of advice I'd offer: Try not to consider money along the way. That, as much as anything, is the most financially sound approach you can take. When you don't consider the money, then you wind up making the right decision. And the right decision almost always leads to money.

It reminds me of the question that somebody once posed to the late great singer Frank Sinatra. "Frank," somebody once asked, "you've got all the money you could possibly want, why are you still singing?" And Sinatra said, "You can't hear money applaud."

Now that we're nearing the end of this book—the end zone, so to speak—you can appreciate how much it takes to be the best. It might sound simple, but it is not easy.

Basically, we are divided into three groups: those who make things happen, those who watch things happen, and those who wonder what happened. It is up to you to decide which one you want to be. You have the opportunity to be as good as you want to be, an idea you should remember through difficult times.

And as I know, there will be plenty of those. Everyone is forced to endure them.

A mother does not enjoy giving birth, but she enjoys *having* given birth. A person does not enjoy exercising, but the person enjoys *having* exercised. A person does not enjoy paying bills, but the person sure enjoys *having* paid bills. If you focus on the reward at the end of your task, it allows you to put more energy into what you're doing. The good ones will sometimes find a way, and the great ones will always find a way.

But as we said at the outset of this project, just as Sean Connery said to Kevin Costner in *The Untouchables,* "What are you prepared to do?" Life is full of choices. You can perform up to the standard or below it. You can work overtime or leave work early. You can choose to have a positive attitude or a negative one.

Now I cannot guarantee that a computer programmer will turn into the next Bill Gates, or an entrepreneur will turn into the next Walt Disney. But this much I can guarantee: If you persist in knocking on the door, your chances of entering the world of success will increase infinitely. And if you *Think Like A Champion,* nothing will stand in your way.

The morning after we beat the Falcons in the Super Bowl, a helicopter whisked me from Fort Lauderdale to Miami Beach for a press conference with the national media. One of the first questions a reporter asked, not surprisingly, regarded the future of the Broncos. He wanted to know if I thought it was realistic to win a third straight Super Bowl title and if so, how we would go about doing it.

"Oh," I told him with a grin, "I have a plan."

Now you do, too. So what are you waiting for? Go show the world how it's done.

PAT BOWLEN

Denver Broncos Owner

First of all, I like to have a good and close relationship with my coach because he's the most important guy in the organization. And with the way we get along, I would be surprised if Mike doesn't finish his coaching career here. If I had to bet on it, I'd say he would.

We have a certain amount of respect for each other. Mike is one of the few individuals I've ever come across—not just in the football business, but in any business—where I'm comfortable letting him do his own thing.

I don't get involved in game plans and this year I never even got involved in the draft. Never spent one minute on it. I didn't even feel it was important for me to be here, in the building for it, because I didn't think I could add one thing to the process. And I didn't think there would be anything that he would do that I would disagree with.

In my mind, in my position, that's a luxury. Having Mike around allows me to perform my other responsibilities with the league and all the things that I do with our new stadium. It's a very warm and comfortable feeling to know that at least part of the organization is well run and as safe as can be.

I have that much trust in him. There's no reason not to. Now, there are things that Mike does that I think are anal. Back in Super Bowl XXXII in San Diego, when we went to the Chargers' facility to practice that week, [Broncos director of operations] Bill Harpole came in to see me and said, "Mike's going to go crazy."

I said, "What do you mean?"

He said, "Well, our facility is right down below a hill."

"So what?"

"Well, Mike's going to think everybody in the world is up there spying on him, taking pictures."

Sure enough, Mike ended up enlisting eighteen special unit Navy SEALS to scour the hill and beat the bushes to make sure no one was up there. Now, these are the same guys who are sent on secret missions into the jungle and never admit to who they are if they're captured. The deal was, they would come out and secure the hill, and then we would take care of them for the game with tickets.

Well, when a news helicopter flew over our practice the first day, Mike went crazy. I think he expected one of these guys to shoot a SAM missile at it and knock it out of the air.

He's also anal about time. He'll come into my office and we'll be having a meeting about something and he'll constantly look at his watch. "Oh, no," he'll say to himself, "it's thirty seconds to one, I've got to be downstairs."

Haven't you noticed that every clock we have in this building, in every room, is the same clock on the same exact time? Coach's locker room, weight room, training room, player's lounge. I once told somebody they were all three minutes slow. Well, that didn't matter. They were all on the same time. And that's the way Mike likes it.

I think when he first got here he drove everybody crazy with that, but not anymore. The players really have grown to accept it and respect it. And I'm not going to criticize him for being anal, because who am I to argue? He has shown what it takes to be the best.

This is my sixteenth year in the football business, and my style has always been to try to give somebody who was working for me all the rope that he needs to do the job—just so long as he doesn't hang himself. People have, but I don't see Mike doing that. He just does too good a job with organization and preparation.

There's not a moment in the day that goes by when Mike doesn't have a plan. He organizes practices, he organizes meals, everything has to happen in a very tight game plan. The difference between him and other coaches that I've worked with in that area is like night and day. The more I see of it, the more comfortable I am that we're going to be extremely successful—unless we hit some bad luck and rotten times—for a long, long time.

I've given him a [seven-year] contract extension already. I might even extend it again. I don't want him going anywhere—ever. It goes without saying that I don't think there's another coach in the league who is as good. You could line them all up and I wouldn't trade Mike Shanahan for any of them.

ACKNOWLEDGMENTS

For helping bring out the best in them, the authors wish to thank:

Cindi Lowe, the best assistant a coach could ever have; Cindy Marshall, the best assistant a writer could ever have; Basil Kane, an agent and friend; Edward and Dorothy Shanahan, parents and role models; Shirley and Jeffrey Schefter, for ceaseless support; Pat Bowlen, whose commitment to be a champion has been unwavering; John Elway, Terrell Davis, Shannon Sharpe, Marcus Allen, Barry Switzer, Deion Sanders, Al Michaels, Joe Montana, George Seifert, Carmen Policy, Matt Millen, Paul Tagliabue, Bill Walsh, Jerry Rice, Tom Jackson, and Steve Young, each of whom was accessible, accommodating, and eloquent; Gerald Grilly, Dennis Britton, Jeanette Chavez, and Neal Scarbrough of the *Denver Post,* who provided the time to help make this happen; Mauro DiPreta, a mastermind editor; Toisan Craigg, a computer whiz; Anja Schmidt, Adrian Zackheim and Lisa Berkowitz, publishing pros; Patrick Falencik, Discount Used Computers' owner; Brady McCombs, who had more research than usual; David Simon, the best friend and copyeditor there is; Jim Saccomano, Paul Kirk, Richard Stewart, and Rebecca Villanueva; Thomas George, always there for advice; Peter King; Greg Aiello; Steven Kaye; Don Kubit;

The Cabo Crew—Tom and Cydney Marsico; Ted and Cindy Halaby; Cindy and Steve Schultz; Oklahoma, Northern Arizona, Minnesota, Florida; Old Navy and Nike.

—MIKE SHANAHAN AND ADAM SCHEFTER

A special thanks to all the loyal players and coaches I've ever worked with and for. This could not have been written without them.

—M.S.